THE 2 AM PRINCIPLE

DISCOVER THE SCIENCE OF ADVENTURE

JON LEVY

Regan Arts.

NEW YORK

Regan Arts.

65 Bleecker Street
New York, NY 10012

First Regan Arts paperback edition, November 2016
Library of Congress Control Number: 2015946537
ISBN 978-1-942872-69-6

Design and illustrations by
Paul Kepple & Max Vandenberg at Headcase Design
www.headcasedesign.com

Printed in China

10 9 8 7 6 5 4 3 2 1

To Hanna & Benjamin Levy

I ask the indulgence of the adventurers who may read this book for dedicating it to two people who mostly stay at home.

I have a serious reason:

They are my parents. They encouraged me as a young boy to live by my own rules and pursue what inspired me. They showed me what it was to risk, to love, and to explore the world even when I was scared to leave home and had no money to do it with.

I have another reason:

They have dared more than any two people I have ever met. They thrust themselves into the unknowns of life and explored the world with no safety net.

I have a third reason:

They loved me no matter how difficult I was and what trouble I caused. Although they now live a quiet life, they inspired the lessons of this book.

If all these reasons are not enough, I will dedicate this book to the adventurers who they were. All of us dream of adventure in our youth, although few of us embrace it as we grow up.

And so I correct my dedication:

To Hanna & Benjamin Levy

When They Were Young

I want to thank Antoine de Saint-Exupéry for creating the words to help me express my appreciation. The words never quite seem enough but hopefully people will hear what can never be captured in language.

THE WARNING I NEED TO GIVE

You are going to have a lot of fun reading this book and learning how easy it is to live a more adventurous life. You will be inspired to have new experiences and participate in outlandish activities. The good news is that most of the adventures you want to have will be great. The bad news is that some of the ideas you come up with will be disastrously terrible.

I know this from experience, having come up with some really awful ideas; in fact, you will read about some of the stupider ones. Most of the time, the bad ones are weeded out, but every so often one gets through the inspection process.

It goes without saying that any risks you choose to take and all of the results are yours and yours alone. They will be a source of pride and embarrassment, and will make phenomenal stories. Just make sure not to do anything too stupid since it can have a serious impact on your life and the people you engage with. If we ever meet or write to each other, I would hope to only hear wild tales of your great successes and embarrassing failures.

THE WARNING I *WANT* TO GIVE

Reading this book may result in adventures that include laughing to the point of tears, nonsensical conversations, toasting with strangers, vague memories of someone saying "You know what would be a great idea..." only to realize, judging by the court summons you find in your pocket in the morning, it really wasn't a good idea, and the odd sense that you may need to get a marriage annulled. Please consult your doctor, lawyer, or priest/rabbi/imam to make sure reading *The 2 AM Principle* is suitable for you.

All These Stories Are True

The stories in this book are all true and accurate to the best of my memory. For years I have made a habit of documenting my adventures, and that, combined with interviewing other participants, is what led to the stories you will read in the pages that follow. When writing this book, I had to make a few difficult choices between being 100 percent accurate and protecting the people you will read about.

Let me reiterate that, in no uncertain terms, all of the stories I share are true. No parts are made-up, but noncritical details may have been changed (such as names, dates and times, locations, etc.). I willingly share these stories knowing that they could affect the way people view me, but I do not wish to bring unwarranted attention to my friends and travel companions. Many of them are very private people or have professional careers for which the outlandish tomfoolery, shenanigans, and ballyhoo that we participated in would be frowned upon.

The only other changes that were made were for the purpose of sharing the stories succinctly. There may be a handful of stories in which the timeline was changed slightly (e.g., I skipped over a stop during the course of a night) so as not to bog down the stories with too many details. Other than that, every story occurred just as it was written. This means every injury, embarrassment, insane invitation, and outrageous conversation was real.

So enjoy my adventures and try not to judge me too much—but if you do, that's fine. Please adventure responsibly.

CONTENTS

STAGE III - INCREASE

STAGE IV - CONTINUE

CHAPTER 1

GET YOUR ESTATE IN ORDER:

YOU MAY NOT BE COMING BACK

SUNDAY, JULY 7, 2013, 8:47 AM GMT +1,

42°48'57.5" N

1°38'21.2" W

Pamplona, Spain

HAD TAKEN THE SAFEST POSITION I could. I was in the front row near the gate, crouched against the sandy floor, my hands protecting my head.

When the gate opened I saw it running at me and I immediately knew I was in trouble. This bull was supposed to enter the stadium by jumping over my head, like the last one, but I wasn't that lucky. It missed its jump.

I felt a sudden sharp pain as its hoof landed on my back, and then nothing but numbness. The screams and cheers of thousands of spectators disappeared, and all I could hear was what sounded like my ribs cracking from the weight of this angry beast. I thought my life was supposed to pass before my eyes in a situation like this, but instead time stopped and the outside world was gone. Was I paralyzed? My brain ordered my limbs to move, but nothing happened.

I had come to the running of the bulls to experience life. Being chased by the bulls into the stadium was one of the most exhilarating moments of my life, but now inside these walls, as the bulls were let in to go toe-to-toe with the runners, I realized this might be the end of it.

I eventually managed to stand up, just barely. As the feeling slowly returned to my body, I could clearly tell my left side had a serious issue, but between the commotion and adrenaline, I couldn't tell what. With the little strength I could muster, I raised my right hand into the air and yelled for help. "*Médico, médico, médico!*" No one was coming to my rescue.

As fate would have it, the 1,500-pound beast that had just hit me wasn't nearly as gentle with my fellow thrill seekers, and in the confusion, all anyone could do to help was drag unconscious and bleeding bodies out of the way.

I knew I had to get somewhere safe before the bull came around for another pass. Someone ran by me and pointed to the edge of the arena where two participants were carrying an unconscious man out for medical attention. I followed them into a room that was being used for triage.

When I entered, a nurse directed me to a bench and started asking questions. The throbbing pain on the top left of my back was growing, making it difficult to pay attention. That coupled with my poor Spanish skills meant I barely understood her, and I probably convinced her I had been hit in the head. As the pain began to overwhelm me, I lost the ability to speak, and I was clearly losing consciousness. All I could do was ask myself, "What was I thinking?"

My friends would say I've developed a knack for getting myself into interesting situations. Actually, it is more like an obsession, born from the desire to refute cultural myths propagated across literature, movies, and TV shows. It may be that when these shared myths were created, the intention was to inspire us to be heroes, to embody values and traits that are considered noble, and to aspire to be better versions of ourselves (more selfless, generous, and compassionate). Unfortunately, over the centuries, as the stories and myths have changed, they have become so aspirational that there is no chance of us living up to their ideals. Instead these great stories have convinced us that an adventurous life is the privilege of merely a handful of personalities or characters who are so ingrained in our cultural mythology they have become cliché.

ARCHETYPE	DESCRIPTION	EXAMPLES
The RAGTAG GROUP	These misfits/outcasts come together and, through their combined talents, overcome some insane obstacle.	*The Hangover, Mission: Impossible, Lord of the Rings, Goonies*
The HERO	A lone man or woman, with an innate skill or power, wields it for the greater good.	Batman, Doctor Who, Sherlock Holmes, Wonder Woman
The DARE-TO-BE-GREAT MOMENT/ THRUST *Into* GREATNESS	An unprepared individual faces adversity but chooses to "take the risk," and in that moment, he/she overcomes a significant obstacle only to discover how extraordinary he/she is.	Daniel in *The Karate Kid,* Katniss in *The Hunger Games,* Bilbo Baggins in *The Hobbit*
The CHOSEN ONE	This person was destined to do great things and has to live up to some pre-existing standard.	Harry Potter, King Arthur, Anakin Skywalker
The BILLIONAIRE PLAYBOY	He lives a life of excitement because of his wealth and is always seeking the next big thrill, yet there is never enough to quench his desire.	Tony Stark, Sterling Archer, Christian Grey

Growing up, I didn't fit into any of these categories. There weren't enough people who wanted to hang out with me to create a ragtag group of misfits. There were no dare-to-be-great moments in which I might save the day, nor was I especially heroic (unless you count the time at age twelve when I ran away from some muggers, but I'd call that more survival instinct than anything else).

In fact, I was really geeky. Nowadays, you can be a cool geek, but back in the early '90s there was no such thing. No one in my school had heard of Steve Jobs, there were no dot-com billionaires, and no sexy tech people made the tabloids. Being geeky meant I would watch lots of science fiction alone and learn computer programming in my spare time. As a child, my class-mates had posters of athletes and cars on their walls, whereas I had Starship Enterprise from Star Trek and comic book superheroes like the X-Men.

One day in eighth grade, my English teacher, deciding to reorganize the seating chart, asked each of us to privately submit two classmates we wanted to sit next to and two whom we refused to sit by. Through an unfortunate series of events I discovered that almost everyone in the class refused to sit next to me. I had hit a new low; I was chubby, nonathletic, and unpopular by almost unanimous vote.

If cultural mythology was right, I was destined for a mundane life. Except for one thing: what I lacked in social skills, I made up for in my desire for excitement and my understanding of science. Beware of a deter-mined geek; we are clever and have very little to lose.

When asked to describe the most wondrous, exciting, and remarkable experiences in their lives, people consistently say they occur by chance, that these experiences are moments of sheer serendipity—a by-product of the universe perfectly aligning to culminate in an extraordinary situation. But if this were true, if it were truly random, we would all live similarly exciting lives, and we don't. This means that there must be some method at work, some best practices that I could learn.

If these best practices could be developed, then I wasn't relegated to being a lonely geek. The upshot of being a wallflower meant I had count-less opportunities to observe and learn. My mission became to understand and develop the ability to live an adventurous life.

Please See Move Information Below

☑ Move completed as requested.

☐ Move NOT completed as requested due to the following reasons:

  ☐ Completed move map was not provided for reference.

  ☐ Destination office is occupied Please contact MS-Move or admin for assistance.

  ☐ Destination office dimensions and/or structural objects would not accommodate requested furniture arrangement

  ☐ Requested furniture is not building standard

  ☐ Computer equipment not connected at origin, not connected at destination.

  ☐ Power/data outlets too far from requested layout. Please contact admin for additional cables, power strips or router/hub.

  ☐ Computer equipment left wrapped for security purposes.

☒ The following items were not moved:

  ☐ Mounted items   ☒ Fridge/(lamp)   ☒ Standard furniture

      ☐ Exposed tech product   ☐ Unlabeled items

☐ For the following reasons:

  ☐ Mounted to wall   ☒ Per RE&F/MS-Move Policy

Comments: _____

_____

Please contact MSIT (425) 706-5000 for assistance with network connectivity and activating additional ports.

Please visit the Facilities Service Center (https://msfacilitites.com/) for cork/ whiteboard/bookshelf requests.

We hope you enjoy your new space!

An adventure, as I see it, is an experience that

1. is exciting and remarkable;

2. possesses adversity and/or risk (preferably perceived risk);

3. brings about personal growth, leaving the participant(s) changed.

UNDERSTANDING THE DEFINITION

You may notice that this book uses a different definition of adventure than what you would find in a dictionary—e.g., "an undertaking usually involving danger and unknown risks."[1] I found this description at once too broad and too specific. Just because an experience possesses danger doesn't automatically make it adventurous, and just because there wasn't danger doesn't mean it wasn't. I needed a definition that worked for everyone, which led to this one. An adventure, as I see it, is an experience that

1. **is exciting and remarkable**. If something is remarkable it means that it is worth talking about. For millenia our species passed on its knowledge and values through an oral tradition of stories, songs, and myths. If the experience wasn't worth talking about, then it wasn't culturally significant. You may have had a nice experience, but if it was not worth discussing, it was not an adventure.

2. **possesses adversity and/or risk (preferably perceived risk)**. If there is no challenge to overcome, then there is neither the chance of success nor failure. Without

---

1 Merriam Webster. S. V. "adventure." www.merriam-webster.com/dictionary/adventure.

adversity or risk, we live stagnant lives that are rather mundane. This is not to say that we need to be in danger. Although the brain processes an imminent threat differently than perceived danger, the physiological responses from both are incredibly similiar.[2] This means you can engage in safe but seemingly dangerous activities and still gain the benefit from a social, physical, and emotional standpoint.

3. **brings about personal growth leaving the participant(s) changed.** No great tale ends with the heroes unchanged; there is always an element of growth. They have expanded their comfort zone and have pushed their social, physical, and emotional boundaries. Their reward is not only the status of success but also the person they have become in the process. Unless you grow from your experiences, you cannot call them adventures.

Unfortunately my progress was painfully slow. Freshman year of high school I made a handful of new friends (though mostly for academic purposes) and spent my free time alone, convincing myself it was to focus on school. Sophomore year, I ventured further and tried to speak to a few girls. Mimicking the popular boys, I several times approached one of the cute girls in my class and attempted to joke around. This seemed like a simple strategy because I saw the popular boys do it every day. I quickly realized, based on the uncomfortable looks and comments I would get, that I wasn't mildly funny or charming. I was living up to my label as an awkward geek.

Luckily, that summer, my mom enrolled me in camp, and in this new environment I was able to reinvent myself. I made several real friends and

2   LeDoux, Joseph. Interview by author. New York, USA and Buenos Aires, Argentina, December 23, 2015.

even had a valentine the following February, although, truth be told, it wouldn't be until freshman year of college that I would kiss a girl.

Over the next fifteen years, humiliating failures eventually paved the way to wondrous nights and wild fun. And that's what brought me to Spain—the thrill of adventure. Unfortunately, I had made an almost fatal mistake. Perceived risk can be just as exciting as actual peril; unfortunately, I underestimated both the danger of this situation and my own incredible stupidity. Seriously, who gets hit by a bull?

Just as my eyes closed, I felt the nurse shake me. I woke from the sudden jolt to see a rather unsympathetic-looking doctor walk over. I explained that when the bull entered the stadium it landed on my left shoulder between my spine and shoulder joint. I couldn't move my shoulder, but my arm and hand were fine.

He took my injured shoulder and began rotating it. I was in visible pain and focused on suppressing the need to scream. I wasn't sure if he was putting a dislocated shoulder back in place, checking for breaks, or finding a cruel way to teach a stupid American a lesson.

He looked at me sternly, chuckled, and said, "It is just a bad bruise; you need to leave now."

A bruise? How could a bruise hurt this much? Fruit bruises, not adventurers. I don't know what was injured more at this point—my shoulder or my ego. Who am I kidding? It was absolutely my shoulder.

I had no right to complain; I was lucky to be alive. Even though I had spent months preparing for the bull run, training daily in cardio and memorizing the path cold, there was one wild animal I underestimated: testosterone.[3] As hormones flooded my system, daring and stupid stunts beyond the run, like approaching the bulls in the stadium and slapping their backsides or allowing the bulls to jump over me, seemed like brilliant ideas, and since I was traveling alone, the only thing that could smack some sense into me was this bull.

It may have taken six months of excruciating physical therapy for my body to recover from the impact, but the incident opened my eyes to something much bigger. In that brief moment right after the bull landed on me, I remember asking myself, "If I am paralyzed, do I regret going on these adventures?" Without a doubt I didn't regret any of it. I embraced my failures, injuries, embarrassments, and even the people who thought I was a

---

3   John Coates. *The Hour Between Dog and Wolf: How Risk Taking Transforms Us, Body and Mind.* (New York, Penguin Books, 2013), 27.

madman. I was proud of the research I had done on adventure, the discoveries I had made, and the person I had become in the process.

So I did the logical thing: I sat down and took stock. In my development from wallflower to world traveler I had not only assembled a collection of best practices, I had begun to see patterns in my experiences. I saw that the best nights almost always involved some kind of preparation. They often involved selecting the right group of people to participate and a new location to explore. There were trends in the types of activities that worked to bring people together, but there also seemed to be a clear line separating a fun night from an extraordinary night that consistently showed up around 2 AM.

TRAVELING ALONE

I know of few experiences that test a person's character more than traveling unaccompanied. You are challenged every moment to make the experience extraordinary and have no one to rely on or blame if it does not meet expectations. It holds a mirror to you, showing you the discrepancy between who you are and who you want to be.

Always remember, when you travel alone you can be anyone you want to be; no one will be there to say otherwise. Note: There are certain circumstances in which traveling alone would be irresponsible. These include scenarios like the running of the bulls, base jumping, night dives, etc., in which there is physical danger and it is important that someone will be there if things go awry.

There is a sound belief that "nothing good happens after 2 AM," that any decision made so late is a reckless, unpredictable one. However, the most epic experiences in my life happened after 2 AM. Whether it was sneaking into a playground with a group of strangers, playing drunken Jenga with Kiefer Sutherland, or taking over a bachelorette party for a wild night on the town, the best parts all happened after 2 AM. That's when I realized the relationship people have with this hour; it is a clear line that makes or breaks an experience, and when someone knows how to traverse it with style, it makes life exciting. Said simply, the 2 AM principle is:

NOTHING GOOD HAPPENS ───── AFTER 2 AM, ─────

EXCEPT

───── FOR THE MOST ─────

EPIC EXPERIENCES OF YOUR LIFE.

After 2 AM, either your night deteriorates into nothing, and the next morning you wake up tired, wondering why you stayed out so late, or it goes in the other extreme, and your night continues to be a thrilling adventure of which tales are told and your friends are envious for years to come.

With this final insight, I realized that traversing this barrier isn't so much an art form as it is a science. I was able to see that each of my most adventurous experiences followed the same four-stage process, and each stage had very specific characteristics that when applied made life exciting.

THE EPIC MODEL OF ADVENTURE

STAGE 1 ESTABLISH	STAGE 2 PUSH BOUNDARIES	STAGE 3 INCREASE	STAGE 4 CONTINUE
Team Location Mission Constraints	Social Emotional Physical	Challenge Surprise Amuse Intrigue	Risk & Unpredictability Activity & Atmosphere Transportation End with Style

I. **ESTABLISH:** The best adventures are by-products of assembling the right elements so that anything can happen, the most important of which involves selecting the right companions and, preferably, a new place to explore.

II. **PUSH BOUNDARIES:** It is essential for participants to get out of their comfort zones and cross a social, physical, or emotional boundary. If the participants are not changed by the experience, they did not go on an adventure.

III. **INCREASE:** The participants maximize their enjoyment by leveraging social characteristics (amusement, intrigue, surprises, and challenges).

IV. **CONTINUE:** Selecting where to go next and how to get there follows a set of simple rules that consider risk, activity, and transportation. Once at the new location, loop back in the process to repeat stages II, III, IV (Push Boundaries, Increase, and Continue again), or End With Style and go home.

Taking the first letter of each stage, the EPIC model of adventure was born. The sum of my experiences and the model I developed told me something loud and clear:

To have an EPIC adventure a person doesn't need to be a hero or thrust into greatness, he or she could simply embrace the 2 AM principle and apply the model.

The only question is: What do you want? When living adventurously, experiences are measured on a grander scale. Successes can be daring masterpieces, but the risks are also greater. Most of the time, no one will get hurt (as long as you stay away from the bulls), but strangers can be unpredictable, new cities have dangerous areas you don't know about, and you can easily beat yourself up over making a mistake. All of these things become amplified when you live a life of adventure.

You have been given a taste of what lies ahead, of countless nights of successes and failures, of risk and discoveries. Now you have a choice to make about your life. Reading this will forever change your standards and expectations. You can't unread or unlearn what you will see here. So you can either put this book down now and walk away, or turn the page and discover how far the rabbit hole really goes. If you are in, buckle up, and hold onto your hat, because we are going on an adventure, and it's going to last the rest of your life.

The choice is yours. Choose wisely.

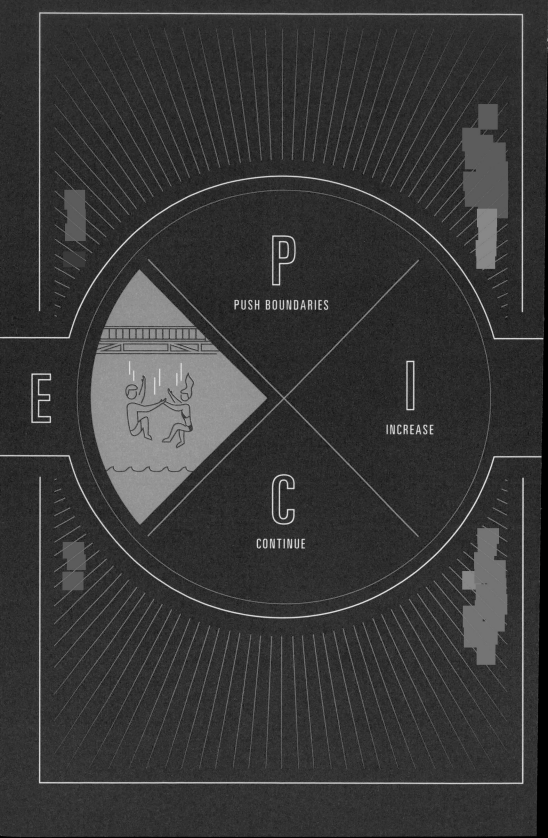

STAGE 1

ESTABLISH

STAGE 1

"BEFORE ANYTHING ELSE,
PREPARATION IS THE KEY TO SUCCESS."
—ALEXANDER GRAHAM BELL

I often hear people say, "Isn't the beauty of adventure that it is unpredictable? That it happens by serendipity or chance?" This may be true for some adventures, but when you put the right elements in place from the beginning, the opportunity that anything can happen (thus creating the impression that everything happened by luck) opens up.

It is not about scripting the experience, since during the course of an adventure opportunities will arise and unforeseen circumstances will create challenges, but what makes it possible to embrace these opportunities and overcome these challenges is that you have established four basic elements: you need the right team, an exciting location (preferably new), an underlying mission to drive the action, and constraints to catalyze creativity.

The fact is that every great adventure begins with these basic elements. Every story, from *The Hobbit* or the *Odyssey* to your craziest night out, had most, if not all, of these characteristics whether you realized it or not. If you think back to your greatest adventure, assuming you weren't alone, weren't you with the right team of people, those who embraced the excitement and pushed you to enjoy yourself? It wouldn't be the same if you went with a lame group of people you hated. You were likely in an unfamiliar environment that was exciting to explore, like a new city or foreign country.

You may have even had an underlying mission to your experience, a goal of some kind that was driving people's participation, and, coupled with that, a set of constraints that limited your options and caused you to be creative or interact with other people.

You will notice that these four characteristics don't dictate how your adventure will go; they just give you the best chances of turning an ordinary experience into an extraordinary adventure worthy of your time.

STAGE I—ESTABLISH
PUT THE RIGHT ELEMENTS IN PLACE

TEAM

Selecting the right people can make a lame experience fun,
whereas the wrong people will make fun experiences miserable.

LOCATION

An exciting location, preferably one you have not been to before,
triggers new behavior and the desire to explore.

MISSION

A goal or objective will bond group members, maintain activity,
and drive interaction.

CONSTRAINTS

Limiting our options actually causes us to enjoy experiences
more. It is in the limitation that we find creative solutions and
can enjoy familiar environments in new ways.

CHAPTER 2

TEAM:

ADVENTURERS, ASSEMBLE!

ONE OF THE MOST IMPORTANT LESSONS I have ever learned was thanks to a single sentence uttered by a mentor of mine. He said, "The quality of our lives is defined by the people we surround ourselves with and the conversations we have with them."

Most of us know this to some degree. If we spend time with athletes we tend to get fit; if we spend time with criminals, it is only a matter of time before we break the law ourselves. In 2009, James Fowler and Nicholas Christakis published a book examining the science of how our social networks affect us.[4] They found that everything from obesity to happiness stems

---

4   James H. Fowler and Nicholas A. Christakis, *Connected: The Surprising Power of Our Social Networks and How They Shape Our Lives* (New York: Little, Brown, 2011).

from and is passed through our networks. The importance of this lesson is that an exceptional life is about curating the people around you. Most people end up with friends based on proximity and coincidence. They went to the same class, worked at the same company, or lived in the same building. These may be lovely and wonderful people, but the true opportunity comes from seeking out people because we admire their character, attitude, and skills.

HAPPINESS, SADNESS, OBESITY, AND EVERYTHING ELSE

In February 2010, Dr. Nicholas Christakis took the main stage of TED and shared a story that made us question the impact of our relationships. Christakis and his research partner, Dr. James Fowler, were curious about the highly popularized topic of the obesity epidemic. Their curiosity was specifically in "whether obesity really was epidemic, and could spread from person to person"[5] like the common cold. Traditional thinking would have us believe that people are obese because of a personal choice, lack of self-control, or genetic disposition. But Christakis and Fowler raised a wild question: What if we contracted obesity? What if it is something that could be transferred from person to person?

Their results were staggering. They discovered that if you have an obese friend, your chances of being obese increase by 45 percent; more surprisingly, your friends who don't know your obese friend have a 25-percent increased chance of obesity just because you are friends with him or her. This effect continues to be felt all the way through three degrees of separation.

This happens for multiple reasons, and to understand it in depth I recommend reading their book *Connected: The*

5   Christakis, Nicholas. "The Hidden Influence of Social Networks." Filmed February 2010. TED Talk, 20:59. www.ted.com/talks/nicholas_christakis_the_hidden_influence_of_social_networks?language=en#t-513809

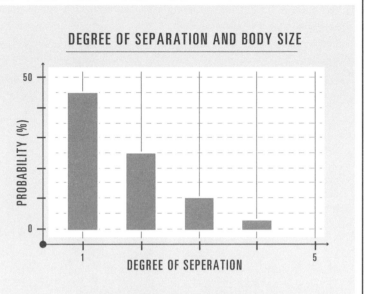

DEGREE OF SEPARATION AND BODY SIZE

PROBABILITY (%)

50

0

1

DEGREE OF SEPERATION

5

*INCREASE IN PROBABILITY THAT A PERSON
IS OBESE GIVEN THAT A SOCIAL CONTACT IS OBESE %*

Surprising Power of Our Social Networks and How They Shape Our Lives, but a simple example of one of the factors would be going to dinner with an obese friend. When you see your friend order significantly more food than you are accustomed to, overindulging becomes more socially acceptable to you. If this happens often, you will develop new habits. In turn, when you go to eat with other friends, you will pass on these habits.

Similarly, Fowler and Christakis discovered that everything from happiness and depression to voting, divorce, and smoking can spread through this superhuman organism we call a social network. The implications are significant, not the least of which is that there is scientific evidence that the people you surround yourself with will define the quality of your life, your friends' lives, and so on. So pick your friends carefully.

My mentor was right: there is no single characteristic that will affect how enjoyable an experience is more than the people with whom you are experiencing it. As a result, when I assemble a group to go out, it sometimes feels like I'm casting a *Mission: Impossible* movie or a bank robbery. I need to make sure that each person is someone I love to spend time with and that he or she brings unique characteristics to our dynamic team.

There are very few absolute rules to group building, but there are some guiding principles I would encourage:

- Diversity of personalities and skills is essential; it gives you the ability to relate to more people you interact with and access to more locations you would want to visit.

- Gender ratio is dependent on where you go and what you want to do. An even mix for social occasions is wonderful, but when exploring nightlife or crashing an event, it is helpful if the ratio leans female or, at most, has just one more man than the total number of women. Most venues are happier when there are more women, and I have often seen groups turned away at clubs because they had too many men. When crashing a party, your group will seem less intimidating if you have more women than men.

- Limit group size or be willing to split up. Larger groups make transportation and location entry difficult, and they also suffer from more delays for bathroom stops, ATM withdrawals, phone calls, etc.

- Members should have a positive attitude. No drama, and no fighting. Nothing ruins fun like unnecessary drama.

SATURDAY, MARCH 28, 2009, 3:26 PM GMT −5,

40°43'51.6" N

73°59'09.3" W

New York, New York, USA

It had been a long week, and I needed to let loose. I had a plan: Four people—two guys and two girls—would go to a random intersection in Manhattan and explore the city. For this, I hand-selected three of the most rambunctious people I could think of. These people would be willing to show up uninvited to a party, embarrass themselves publicly, or approach strangers without hesitation. The lineup was:

1. **Q:** The brains. The type of girl who is always on her toes, always watching the crowd and eager to meet people.

2. **Lulu:** The smoldering minx. The kind of woman who brings men to their knees, opens doors, and could handle people of any social status we came in contact with.

3. **Whiplash:** The outrageous extrovert. A male counterpart I could trust to play me up and manage the group whenever I'm not around.

4. **Me:** The point man. I would guide the group and set down all the groundwork.

So the texts went out: "Prepare yourself . . . We have an adventure tonight, 21:00 hours, debauchery will ensue."

Whiplash and Lulu were in; unfortunately Q had plans she couldn't get out of. We were down a girl. I had two options: either review my list of backup team members or make some friends wherever we ended up. The second option sounded a lot more interesting.

LET FATE DECIDE

When you can't decide where to go or what to do, or would like to add an element of excitement to your night, toss the metaphorical die. Set a timer, flip a coin, ask strangers, etc., but whatever system you use, take the decision completely out of your hands. You need to be fully committed to what the results are unless they are dangerous. You'll find it's an unbeatable way to get out of your routine.

I wanted to be surprised by where we went that night; not knowing prevented us from planning, which added a sense of excitement. So when the three of us met up and got into a cab, I told the driver to head downtown and east. I set the timer on my phone for ten minutes, and wherever we were when it hit zero, we would get out.

When we got out of the cab, it took us a moment to orient ourselves. We were on Twelfth Street and Second Avenue and looking for somewhere to grab some dinner. I noticed a restaurant nearby with a facade made entirely of glass. Two attractive women were sitting inside by the window having drinks. As we approached to read the menu hanging on the glass, I waved hello. They smiled and waved back. Without missing a beat, Whiplash ran to the window and touched the glass, recreating the classic scene from *E.T.* in which they touch fingers; the taller of the two pressed her finger to the glass, reciprocating. These two were obviously very playful and open to engaging with us.

Within seconds, we were inside, introducing ourselves and sharing their guacamole and chips. They were friendly, cute, and in their late twenties. I was happy Lulu was there; it was obvious the inclusion of an attractive girl in our group put them at ease.

When we began to chat, they were clearly ill-prepared for the craziness we were about to introduce into their lives. The taller one immediately asked us, "So, what do you all do?"

LITMUS TESTS

During your adventures, it is important to be able to quickly assess whom you will mesh with and who is a poor fit for interaction. I recommend the use of litmus tests. Named after the strips of color-changing paper schoolchildren use in science class to test whether something is acidic, neutral, or basic, these tests are ideal as they require little to no effort and provide a quick result. To figure out what type of person you're dealing with, put forward the appropriate litmus tests. For example:

- Openness: Smile and wave to strangers to see if they wave back
- Playfulness: Ask, "What is the craziest thing you ever did on a dare?"
- Creativity: Ask, "If you could invent an Olympic sport, what would it be?"
- Daring: Ask, "What was the last thing you did that scared you?"

Depending on the types of personalities you want to engage with, make sure to develop the right litmus tests. It will save you from awkwardness and disappointment later in the experience.

While I answered, I signaled Lulu and Whiplash to pull up chairs. If these women hadn't wanted us there, they wouldn't have engaged us with questions. Getting into a conversation about what all of us do meant we were going to be there at least another five or ten minutes.

I asked the shorter girl if she had ever used an iPod. "Yes, of course," she responded.

Making up the most ridiculous career I could think of, I explained that I had the world's most average ears and that companies like Bose, Panasonic, and Sony base their headphones off of them. In fact she had me to thank for the comfort of her headphones.

"Oh cool," she said. Then she asked about Whiplash.

I was in a bit of shock that she bought it.

Whiplash said he was a before-and-after fitness model for late-night infomercials. Whereas my story was a litmus test to see how gullible these girls were, Whiplash's story was true.

Lulu then chimed in with her background: "I'm a second-generation carnie. My mother was an acrobat with the European Vaudeville Circus, and my father was an Australian singer–turned–casino executive. After I got my master's in writing and statistics, I began working for an international counterterrorism organization."

The girls' jaws dropped; they couldn't make sense of what Lulu had just shared. That was Lulu for you—no matter what I made up, when she told the truth I just couldn't compete.

When you bring together interesting people, they have a social gravity to them that naturally draws people in. Lulu was one of those people; she wasn't just a pretty face. She was passionate about whatever she did, which inspired people, and she never judged anyone, which made people feel very comfortable around her. This kind of personality is amazing for group building because it is fun and impressive without making others feel inferior.

Unsurprisingly, after Lulu's self-description, the girls invited us to stay for dinner.

Eventually the conversation turned to the girls' occupations. The taller one was a lawyer and the other worked as a real estate broker. I wanted the two of them to come along for the rest of the night; they were fun and they put the gender ratio in much better shape. To get the evening going a little faster, I ordered a round of shots for table. I'm always impressed by how people bond over taking shots together.

As a way to encourage people to participate in crazy antics, I look for an opportunity to compliment the person or group on having an adventurous attitude and their willingness to embrace exciting opportunities. The key is to get them to identify with that trait so that later when they are invited to participate in some activity, they will embrace it as part of who they are.

When the shots arrived, we raised our glasses and I made a toast: "To our new friends: It is an honor to be dining with two people who are so adventurous and open to new opportunities. Everyone talks about seizing the day, but you two embrace opportunities as they come. To tonight and many more nights of adventure. Cheers!!"

INTERRUPTING THE AVERAGE NIGHT

If you look at most nights people have, they tend to be predictable and unremarkable. People often go to the same places, participate in the same activities, and have the same conversations. Some love their routine and wouldn't want to change it, but many of us enjoy an interesting interruption to life.

To be very clear, if you strike up a conversation with a stranger at a bar, talk to a couple at a restaurant, or insert yourself into the middle of a group traveling down the street, you are still interrupting, but you are often a welcome interruption.

If you are fun and have interesting stories and ideas, it will be exciting for the people you meet. You are like a winning lottery ticket to a fun life, and if they hold onto you, they will have an adventure they will tell their friends about for years to come.

If it is not a good match, if you don't find them interesting or they don't want to be interrupted, you simply excuse yourself. They will go about their average night, and you will find some cohorts who are up for excitement elsewhere.

And like that, I knew they were in.

As we were all chatting, sharing stories, and eating, people kept looking in and reading the menu hanging on the glass. Building on our previous success, we would wave and signal them to come in.

Eventually two Turkish men accepted the invitation. Unfortunately there was something a little low-spirited about them, and it quickly became clear what. One of them shared that he had just gone through a tough breakup and was suffering from depression. As much as I felt for this person, I didn't know him and my responsibility was to my friends.

Whiplash, now deep in conversation with the lawyer and the broker, flashed a look of concern. We had to ditch the guys.

Whenever you speak with strangers, you take the risk that they won't mesh well with your group. You can typically figure this out with a few litmus tests before committing significant time. If the person isn't a good match, you can initiate an escape.

I shook the men's hands and said, "Gentlemen, it was a pleasure meeting you, but we need to catch up with our friends. I hope you have a wonderful night. Take care." They politely walked out.

It was now time to find another place to go. I sifted through the Facebook invites on my phone, and I came across a house party a few blocks away.

We closed our check and invited the girls to come, promising them a great party. The lawyer said she had to be at work the next morning, but agreed to come for one quick drink before she had to leave. Every time I hear people say this I laugh because I have never known anyone to actually only have one drink and then leave. Not to mention, we had just complimented her on how she embraces exciting opportunities; she would feel silly if she didn't live up to it.

THE ART OF THE ESCAPE

It is quite common to find yourself in a situation in which you need to escape a boring person/conversation or get rid of a social barnacle (someone who sticks to you and won't let go).

There is a careful balance to be struck between being considerate and wasting your time. I tend to be very direct and friendly with people since I don't want to mislead anyone. To accomplish this, I smile, make eye contact, and use what is known as a politician's handshake. It is a handshake designed to create a greater sense of relatedness and trust. Your right hand is in a strong shake, while your left hand is either on the person's shoulder, above the elbow, or grasping the outside of their right hand.

Then I say one of the following:

TO WALK AWAY GRACEFULLY, I SAY,

- "You will have to excuse me, I promised that I would speak to someone here and I have to go. I hope you have a wonderful evening."
- "It was a pleasure meeting you. Unfortunately I have to take care of a call, email, etc. . . . Please excuse me." Then pull out your phone as you walk away and stare at it, avoiding eye contact.

TO GET RID OF PEOPLE, I SAY,

- "It was great meeting you, but we were planning on spending quality time with our friends and catching up. Take care."

> - "You will have to excuse us, we were planning on catching up alone for a while. I hope you have a wonderful evening."
> - "Please pardon us. I need to discuss a rather personal matter with these people. I wish you only the best."
>
> Notice that I never provide a full explanation; frankly, it is no one's business, and the longer you speak, the more a person can be pulled into a conversation. It is short, clean, and friendly.

Do you know those classic moments in movies when people walk into a party? The camera pans across the house, and you see all the cool, sexy, popular people hanging out talking and drinking?

Well, they definitely didn't film it at this party. Looking across the room all we saw was a group of clueless overweight tech guys in their late twenties. I laughed to myself. I had convinced these girls I would take them for a wild night, and I had brought them to what looked like a tech conference.

Luckily this party had two things going for it. The host had a stocked top-shelf bar. And more important, it had us. I would always rather be with the right people at the wrong party than with the wrong people at the right party. If you are with the right people you can always turn a party around, but the right party won't make the wrong people fun.

Lulu pulled out her iPhone and plugged it in, replacing the classic rock with the hottest new pop music. If a pretty woman changes the music, there isn't a man alive who would argue with her.

I tossed Whiplash a cocktail shaker off the table. "Drinks and shots for everyone," I told him.

Mickey, the host, walked over and gave me a huge hug, the kind of hug that said, "Thank you for bringing some cool people with you." I smiled.

He turned to the group and asked, "So what are you drinking? We have vodka, rum, absinthe, gin, and tequila—but the tequila is just for body shots."

On hearing tequila, the lawyer perked up. "Let's go!"

Before the words were out of her mouth, Whiplash was already pouring shots of tequila. He never missed an opportunity to escalate things.

By the time each of us had a shot in our hands, Mickey was already sucking the lemon out of the lawyer's face. Without hesitation, he lay down on his couch, put a lemon in his mouth, pulled up his shirt, and placed the shot glass on his belly button. The rest of us were stunned, not just by how ballsy Mickey was, but that he had so much body hair it looked like he had a sweater on under his shirt. I gagged a little thinking about taking a shot from his belly button. That lawyer must have really loved tequila. As she took her shot off of Mickey, the rest of us toasted them, hoping that the burn of the alcohol would cleanse us of what we had just seen.

SELECTING THE RIGHT DRINK

Drink association: Culturally, we have developed associations with various types of alcohol and their social implications. Think about how often people drink piña coladas on a beach/pool vacation but almost never in a bar in the middle of winter. Some drinks are viewed as more intimate (whiskey), some are celebratory (champagne or sparkling wine), and others are about bonding and debauchery (tequila shots). When making a drink suggestion, consider the frame of mind you want to put people in.

Order fast: Always have a go-to drink. It is insanely annoying when you are placing a drink order and someone is being indecisive and holding up the process. This issue is magnified when it is difficult to get a bartender's attention, and if you don't order quickly, he or she could walk away. So figure out a drink you like, and when you have to make a quick decision, just go with it.

Mickey offered the lawyer a "tour" of the apartment. I couldn't believe it—for the first time in my life someone had managed to do it. She really did have only one quick drink and then left us for her private "tour" with Mickey.

With our host occupied, Whiplash and I took it upon ourselves to entertain the guests, but after forty-five minutes, it was time for us to move on. We had had our fun and the novelty was wearing off.

The moment we exited the front door, we saw a limo blaring music with a three-foot-long inflatable penis hanging out the window. I ran after it with Whiplash, Lulu, and the broker behind me. When I reached the limo, I asked if I could hop in. They nodded, and the four of us piled in on the floor while the limo was moving. You know you brought together the right group of people when you have a crazy opportunity like this and they don't hesitate to take action. When I started running after the limo, I clearly had no sane plan, but the others started running just a few feet behind me, ready to take on whatever came next.

We were now a pile of drunken, uncoordinated bodies on the floor of a stretch limo surrounded by six beautiful women who, based on the collection of penis paraphernalia that they were wearing, were celebrating a bachelorette party.

"So what's the next stop?" I asked.

One of the girls said a club I hadn't heard of and followed it with a "Woo!" From the sound, they were clearly ready to celebrate. A few minutes later the limo stopped, someone opened the door from the outside, and all ten of us were ushered into what could only be described as a second-rate hip-hop club. The surprised looks on the women's faces suggested that the club was not exactly what they were expecting. It was clear that we were going to have to relocate the group.

I had a backup plan. I knew a handful of clubs and lounges that would have been happy to host us, including Bukaru right across the street. In order to relocate, I knew the bachelorette had to be taken care of, since it was her special night, and that the group needed to feel like they got their money's worth from a $250 bottle of vodka.

So Whiplash and I took over the table, we mixed and poured, and they were all happy, dancing, and out the door in forty minutes, off to Bukaru across the street.

RELOCATING A GROUP

Moving a group is a complex procedure involving considerations ranging from weather and attire to desired experience and distance. This is covered in full detail in Stage IV—Continue. Until then, here are a few pointers on selecting a place to move a group.

- **There's an app for that**: There are countless mobile apps that will list and rate venues based on your location. Just because something has a high or low rating doesn't make it good or bad; it depends on who is rating it and what type of experience you want to have.

- **Ask security/staff**: People who work in nightlife tend to know other nightlife people and venues. Not only can they suggest a good location, they will also often know someone who works there.

- **Ask patrons**: Chances are good that other people in the venue know the area. Find the people with the best vibe and ask them. It is also a great way to meet people and take them along with you.

- **Take the right path**: If you are changing location, take a path that will bring you by other potential venues so you can check out other places on the way. There is no harm in going on a venue crawl.

Moving eight drunk women across several lanes of traffic in the middle of the night was pure chaos but worth the inconvenience. At Bukaru, the velvet ropes opened up, and we were quickly seated at a table. Vodka and champagne poured like water, and everyone couldn't have been happier.

We danced, we drank, and as the numbers dwindled, I sat back and marveled at the night we had all created. When I sent out the text that morning, I couldn't have imagined we would have crashed a dinner, taken over a house party, introduced my friend to a cute girl, jumped into a moving limo, crashed a bachelorette party, finished off table service at one club, and gotten a free table at another. It was really true: the quality of our life is defined by the people we surround ourselves with. When you bring together a group of extraordinary people, you will get extraordinary results.

I smiled to myself thinking, "Not a bad night for a lowly ear model. Well, maybe not lowly. After all, I do have the world's most average ears."

TAKEAWAYS:

☑ Curate the people around you. There is nothing more important to an adventure than surrounding yourself with the right people.

☑ If you've chosen well, the right people will turn a bad experience around, while a bad group will make potentially great experiences awful.

☑ Invite strangers to join you. If they are a good fit, you will have made a new friend; if they aren't, you can go your separate ways.

☑ Use litmus tests to make sure you're interacting with the right people.

CHAPTER 3

LOCATION:

JUST ANOTHER MONDAY

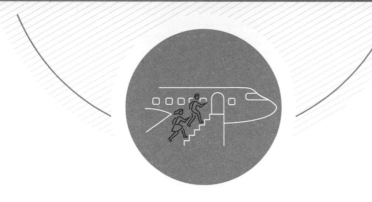

HOW MANY OF THE DAYS IN the last week do you remember? What about the last month? If you are like most people I ask, you will describe a handful, mostly the day a big project was due or a weekend when you went to a friend's party. Maybe you will come up with five or six if you rack your brain for a while. But why is that? Why is it that so little of our life stands out? It's likely due to the fact that we tend to follow routines. We drive the same way to work every day, hang out with the same people at lunch, go to the same restaurants, order the same meals, sit in the same seats, visit the same stores, watch the same shows, and even have the same conversations.

When most days follow a routine, they blend together, and we have no reason to remember them.

Routines are by no means a bad thing; they are essential to developing healthy habits for everything from exercise to work productivity, but for the most part, they do not lead to a stimulating and remarkable life.

In light of this, one of the most effective ways to make an experience more exciting is to go somewhere you have never been. The fact is, I have never heard of a great adventure taking place in someone's home or back-yard unless it involved a group of five-year-olds.

Our brains respond differently to new environments. Without the ability to fall back on previous knowledge, our brains develop new neural pathways as we learn about and make sense of the new environment. Otherwise dormant sections of our brains activate, releasing a mix of chemicals to absorb all the new sights, smells, and sounds, and then attempt to make sense of them all. You will notice that in this hyperaware state, we become conscious of and open to new opportunities to explore.[6]

ROUTINE IS THE ENEMY OF

EXCITEMENT!

AUTHOR'S TIP:

We don't always have the option to go to another city or country, but we generally have the option to go to a new bar, restaurant, area of town, music venue, or person's house, or to participate in an activity that we usually would pass over.

---

6 Cell Press. "Pure Novelty Spurs The Brain." ScienceDaily. www.sciencedaily.com/releases/2006/08/060826180547.htm (accessed January 11th, 2016.).

THE NOVELTY CENTER

Looking to better understand how the brain responds to novelty, Nico Bunzeck of University College London and Emrah Düzel of University College London and Otto von Guericke University conducted a series of experiments examining a section of the brain which has been referred to as the "major 'novelty center'" called the SN/VTA (Substantia Nigra/Ventral Tegmental Area).[7]

Bunzeck and Düzel ran an experiment in which people's brains were scanned using fMRI (functional magnetic resonance imaging) technology while they were shown several images of the same thing (a face or outdoor scene). Inserted among the familiar images were four types of different, or "oddball," faces or scenes. By varying the content of oddball images, researchers were able to see how the brain responds to the unique content.

In a similar oddball experiment, researchers presented subjects with images that varied in levels of familiarity and novelty. Bunzeck and Düzel determined that the "SN/VTA novelty responses were scaled according to absolute rather than relative novelty in a given context."[8] This means that the more novel something was the greater the response. Additionally, "this novelty motivates the brain to explore, seeking a reward."[9]

The importance of a new location is clear; the brain activates areas dedicated that induce exploration, learning, and reward when the environment is new and novel. These areas are not activated in the same way when you are in a familiar environment and experience.

---

7   Nico Bunzeck and Emrah Düzel. "Absolute coding of stimulus novelty in the human substantia nigra/VTA." *Neuron*, 51 no. 3 (2006): 369–79.

8   Ibid.

9   Cell Press. "Pure Novelty Spurs the Brain.".

There are certain rules I try to live by that I would encourage you to adopt:

1. **SAY YES! If you are invited to something, even something that isn't your style, say yes.** Nothing truly interesting or exciting happens at home; if it did, we wouldn't own TVs, and everyone would just try to come over to your place every day, and they would pay to get in.

2. **Go to events and activities you would never normally go to.** If you keep going where you always go, you will have a progressively less interesting experience over time. We get desensitized and the novelty wears off. Check out events and experiences that are completely foreign to you (e.g., a biker festival, a transvestite fashion show, a Civil War reenactment, a pie-eating contest, etc.). And don't be afraid to participate. It is important to try a variety of experiences. You may not love them all, but they will still be more interesting and amusing than staying at home.

3. **Keep a list of interesting places in your area.** And make sure you always have a trip to one of them planned in advance.

4. **Don't be fooled by misattribution.** People have a tendency to attribute an experience to a place and then fall in love with it, continuously wanting to go back thinking that every time you go back it will be equally enjoyable. Just because I had an amazing experience somewhere once doesn't mean it will always be great. The likelihood is that it will become less exciting over time.

You should leave now, your life depends on it. If you want to live a life worth remembering and participate in activities that push you and make you grow, you need to get out right now. Don't waste any more time. You deserve an extraordinary life, and it won't happen if you are on your couch watching reality TV.

THE EXPLORER'S PERSPECTIVE

There is a critical shift in mindset that anyone aspiring to an adventurer's lifestyle should embrace. As you explore new locations, leave your expectations at home; they will only serve to disappoint you and prevent you from enjoying yourself.

Once people develop expectations,

1. they are less likely to notice other opportunities, since their minds are focused on preconceived notions;

2. they spend their time evaluating whether the experience they are having matches these expectations. Since they are often based in fantasies people create, reality will often fail to match the expectations.

This means that as we venture out, we need to separate novelty from fun. At times new places will be fun, other times they will be boring, scary, offensive, or even dangerous. We have a tendency to believe that something novel will be exciting and enjoyable, but no one can guarantee that. Many times, the adventure is in discovering that where you go is terrible and you need to turn things around. Other times, you will discover an entire world and culture that inspires you to think differently and experience new things. Regardless, leaving your expectations at home and coming with the perspective of an explorer who wants to see what there is to learn and to try will provide the most enjoyment.

MONDAY, JULY 7, 2014, 1:13 AM GMT +2,

Eilat, Israel

29°32'59.9" N

34°57'37.0" E

Elsa looked over to me in midair. All she could think was, "How am I still falling!?!?!"

When we decided to jump off the bridge, she thought it would only take a second to hit the water. She was partially right, but what she hadn't accounted for was that when your body is pumping with that much adrenaline, you think faster, and everything around you seems to move slower. This meant she had enough time to have a panicked conversation with herself, exploring the not-so-minor question of why she hadn't hit the water yet.

If we timed our jump right, we would be able to land in the water, swim to shore, push our way through the gathering crowd of shocked and envious onlookers, put our clothes back on, and run off to safety before the cops caught up with us.

To even begin to comprehend how completely insane it was for Elsa to be bridge jumping with me, it is important to understand how we met.

DON'T CAUSE TROUBLE IN YOUR CITY

I can't emphasize this enough. I cross a lot of social boundaries when I travel. In fact, I probably break a lot of local laws in the cities I visit, but what I won't do is go too crazy in the city where I live. You have to be very careful about your reputation since you don't want people in your social circle, venue owners, bouncers, or law enforcement officials to see you in a negative light. You could get yourself blacklisted or alienated within your own community. You have to decide for yourself where to draw the line. I believe in pushing limits, but be careful of what you do in your backyard.

When you do cause trouble, know the local laws. If you are going to break the law, make sure you know the consequences; you don't want to find out that whatever country you are visiting has insanely strict laws and end up getting caned, heavily fined, or imprisoned for something that wouldn't be a big deal back home.

THURSDAY, JULY 3, 2014, 5:17 AM GMT +1,

Stockholm, Sweden

59°39'07.2" N
17°56'04.2" E

My best friend, Liam Alexander and I were going through duty-free in Stockholm's Arlanda airport, picking out a few gifts to bring to Israel, where we would meet up with my family for a reunion. We were being our usual friendly selves, which was only accentuated by the fact that we had left the nightlife of Stockholm not an hour and a half before.

As we approached the checkout line, I noticed the rather beautiful girl sitting behind the counter. I flashed a smile, trying to see if she would reciprocate. She grinned a little and asked for my ticket to ensure I was leaving the European Union. When I passed it to her, she unexpectedly lit up and commented on the fact that I was going to Israel.

There was something so sweet about her—an ease and charm that I wanted to get to know—so I asked her if she wanted to come. She explained that she would love to but that she was a graduate student and had to save money.

Without hesitation, I made her an offer: "Would you come if I paid for your trip?"

It took me a second to realize what I had just said; I hadn't really thought about it before I blurted it out. Frankly, I hadn't budgeted for that, but once I heard myself, I knew it was something I wanted to do. I wanted to know myself as the type of person who makes wild promises for the sake of adventure, and sometimes that means figuring things out as they unfold. There were countless cons, but all I needed was one good pro. I get to be the guy who lives a life less ordinary, someone for whom the standard rules don't apply, someone who challenges convention and reason.

She looked at me with an intense gaze, tilting her head as if trying to assess

BE A BETTER YOU

When we are in a foreign environment, we have an opportunity to express and explore aspects of our personalities that would otherwise lie dormant. In a new location, we have no one's expectations to live up to and nothing to prove. You can be anyone, say almost anything, or act in almost any way you want, and there are few social ramifications, if any. It is a social playground where you get to discover facets of who you are in new ways. The question you should be asking yourself is:

WHO DO I WANT TO KNOW MYSELF AS?

Do you want to be the person who buys a stranger a drink just to be nice? Dressed in a tux to explore the city? Spends nights telling tales at a local pub? Dresses down and stays in a hostel even though you have money? Sneaks into a local university to take classes even though you're not a student? Attends an open audition for a Broadway show even though you can't sing?

Whatever it is, you should feel free to try new styles, traits, and ideas. It will never be as easy to create yourself anew as when you are in a new location. You may discover that you don't enjoy the new trait or style, or you may discover a whole new aspect of your identity that you love.

Either way, enjoy the freedom of an environment with few social consequences.

if I was dangerous or even serious. The pause was so long I worried I was coming off as creepy and insane. As a smile developed on her face, she finally broke the silence.

"Yes."

I immediately pulled out my phone, opened the Kayak mobile app, and started searching for flights. Meanwhile, her line filled with more customers; clearly, we were causing a commotion. She was trying to ring people up, I was trying to get flight details, and Liam took on the role of bag boy to expedite the checkout process. As if the situation wasn't odd enough, all her co-workers were now looking at us, wondering what was happening, which in turn led all of the customers in the other checkout lines to stare at us.

I was making progress matching flight dates, until one of the customers began to reprimand Liam for his bag-boy skills: "I must bag my own things," he shouted. "This is a security risk; you could be putting anything in my bag. You aren't allowed to be doing this!"

Worried that I was about to get this lovely girl fired, I agreed to meet her during her break at the restaurant across from duty-free. Twenty-five minutes later, we were figuring out her itinerary, and that's when it hit me: I still had no idea what name I should enter when we purchased the ticket.

BE RESPECTFUL OF PEOPLE'S LIVELIHOOD

When I travel, I speak to everyone—oftentimes people who work in retail because they know the area and may want to hang out when they finish their shift. Many of these jobs can be monotonous, so an interaction with a gregarious person is a lot of fun for them, but you have to remember two things:

1. They are paid to speak to customers and be polite. This may mean they don't really want to talk or interact with you, but they have to.

2. They could get in trouble, reprimanded, or even fired for your behavior.

This means be charming, fun, silly, daring, etc., but be respectful of the fact that they aren't on an adventure yet.

I had somehow convinced a complete stranger to fly to another continent with me, to a city that was being bombarded by missiles, without ever knowing her name. I had done a lot of wild things over the years, but I had no idea if this latest antic was brilliant or crazy. What kind of person says yes to an invitation like this? They are either insanely adventurous or just insane. I have either met a future best friend or invited a crazy woman to spend a week with my nieces and nephews.

After one of the most unexpected interactions of my entire life, we properly introduced ourselves. Her name was Elsa, and as quickly as we met, Liam and I had to run to board our flight. If all went according to plan, Elsa would be arriving in Israel the next evening, giving her time to pick up her passport, leave her job, and pack. Between now and then, I would have to find a way to explain to my parents who this random Swedish girl staying with us was.

FRIDAY, JULY 4, 2014, 11:32 PM GMT +2,

Ein Hod, Israel

I sat there in my parent's living room, anxious for Elsa's arrival. My mind was racing with doubts and worries. Who is this woman? She has no Facebook account and a name so common that nothing shows up on Google. Will she even show up? Do I really want her to show? Sure, it would make an outlandish story, but will it be fun? I was working myself into a frenzy. My normally calm demeanor resembled that of a teenager about to take a final rather than that of a seasoned traveler about to hang out with a new friend.

Ultimately, it was a waste of time to indulge in these questions. The die had been cast, and I would need to focus on making the experience as enjoyable as possible, regardless of whether she didn't show, showed and was lovely, or showed and was a complete lunatic.

Within minutes of her arrival, my family loved her. Elsa won the kids over with Swedish candy and the adults with stories of her studies and growing up in Sweden. It turned out she was so enticed to come to Israel because she was getting her master's in Middle Eastern studies. All this time I thought it was my good looks and charm that had brought her over, but actually she just wanted to see the Holy Land.

By the next day, she was a fully integrated part of the family. She helped set up the family reunion, took the kids to play games, helped prepare lunch with my mom and siblings, and even sat with my father as he painted.

But this was only the first stop of many: over the next week, my family and I took her barhopping in Tel Aviv, to the lost city of Petra in Jordan, and to a dolphin sanctuary in Eilat. We watched the sun rise over the Judean desert and were woken up by sirens and explosions as the Iron Dome protected us from Hamas rockets.

On the fourth day of our trip, we were in Eilat, a resort city in the south of Israel. Liam and I walked into Elsa's room and saw her wiping tears from her face. She was one of those people who never wanted to burden anyone with her issues, but clearly something was weighing heavily on her. We sat with her on the floor, and she confided in us something I could only describe as the nightmare she was dealing with back in Sweden. It turned out that her father was dying of Lou Gehrig's disease (also known as ALS or Amyotrophic Lateral Sclerosis). He was living with her mother, but every few weeks he was in and out of the hospital as the disease slowly took his life. We hugged her, not knowing what to say. Our lives were far from perfect, but neither of us could imagine the pain she was going through. She thanked us. This trip was the first thing she had done for herself in as long as she could remember. She had been so anxious, sad, and stressed about her father that she couldn't enjoy herself in Sweden. Everything back home served as a reminder of her father's illness and what her family had to endure. This trip was the break she needed so she could actually have some fun.

DON'T WAIT FOR MAGIC—

CREATE IT!

AUTHOR'S TIP:

A NEW LOCATION, A NEW START

When struggling with an issue, it can be therapeutic to go somewhere new. I'm not talking about running away from a problem so much as putting yourself in a new environment to get some perspective and process the issue. You might have experienced a tough breakup, a death in the family, or another tragedy. It can be beneficial to get away for a bit:

- A new location won't have all the history and reminders of what you are struggling with.
- The novelty and people can distract you, allowing you to process what you need to in a steady and healthy way.
- You gain perspective from seeing the issues others deal with.
- It gives you permission to experience joy.

Note: I am not a medical professional and cannot advise you on proper courses of therapy.

After hearing about Elsa's father, Liam and I made it our mission to give her the most magical trip of her life. I had a fun idea. Nothing makes you feel alive like challenging your fears and coming out on top. When I had been to the boardwalk of Eilat as a child, I had seen people jumping several stories off a bridge into water. It was time for Elsa to shake things up. It was time for her to experience bridge jumping.

That evening, I took Elsa and Liam to explore the boardwalk of Eilat. Crossing that bridge I had remembered from childhood, I saw a sign: "DANGER!!! Jumping off the bridge is strictly forbidden!" Seeing no boardwalk patrols nearby, I turned to Elsa and said, "I'm going to need you to trust me now. I'm stripping down to my underwear and passing all of my clothing to Liam. I think you should too."

She was obviously confused, but having spent the better part of a week with me, she knew whatever I had planned was going to be worth it. Passers-by started noticing our odd behavior and stared at us, a common occurrence for the three of us by now. I took her by the hand and led her to the middle of the bridge, where I started climbing over the safety railing. She looked at me with a wide-eyed mixture of terror and excitement, realizing what was about to happen.

Meanwhile, a large crowd gathered in anticipation of our jump. As we crossed the barrier, my hands began to shake, and my legs felt like Jell-O. Her voice cracked a little when she broke the silence: "Are we really doing this?"

Ignoring her question, I told her, "The key is not to hesitate. The longer we wait, the scarier it will be, so we are going on the count of three. One, two, three!"

Before we had the time to doubt ourselves, we were midair, falling rapidly toward the water. I looked over to her, trying to read her face, but by the time I could make sense of anything, I was already underwater trying to get to the surface. We swam to shore, scaled the rocks, pushed through some of the onlookers, and grabbed our clothes from Liam. By the time we were dressed, Liam had already jumped off the bridge and was ready to start running to the far side of the boardwalk, to avoid getting in trouble with the cops.

As we sat for a round of celebratory drinks, we realized that Elsa's demeanor had changed completely. She was wet, messy, and dirty, but she was a new person, high on the experience of pushing boundaries and challenging her fears. She was in a new place, with new friends, experiencing new challenges. She was alive and happy.

At the end of the trip, as Elsa was getting in her cab to the airport, she asked me a wonderfully sweet question that seemed to sum up the entire week: "Since the day we met, I have been curious: Why me? There are countless pretty women out there. Why did you choose me?"

She had such a modest nature that I don't think she could have ever expected my response. I explained: "The simple answer is, because you said yes. The full answer is, no one says yes to such an outrageous invitation; it takes a very special person. I meet a lot of people who talk about

THE OPEN-DISTANCE SCALE

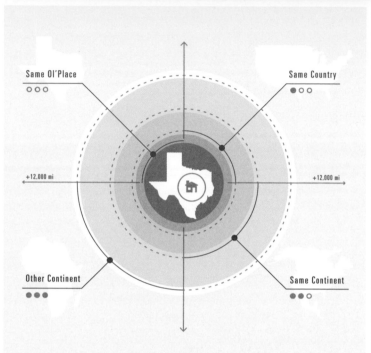

Same Ol'Place ○○○

Same Country ●○○

+12,000 mi

+12,000 mi

Other Continent ●●●

Same Continent ●●○

You will notice that the farther someone is from home the more open they are to:

1. connecting quickly with strangers;

2. engaging in activities that they would never participate in back home.

CONNECTING

It is human nature to be social beings. We have a need to connect, and when our environment is foreign, we can feel isolated, alienated, and homesick. Experience tells me that in this state, people open up much faster. As you travel, you will notice how easily a friendly hello and a smile start a conversation. This is especially true when there is a shared language or culture that is distinct from the environment. Two Americans meeting in China are much more likely to connect than the same two meeting in Chicago. Considering this phenomenon, you should feel comfortable saying hello to anyone you come across and then focus on finding as much common ground as possible. It is one of the reasons I like to travel alone; chances are there will always be friendly people wherever I go.

EXPERIENCES

Similar to the openness, I have found that the farther people are from home, the more likely they are to participate in activities that would be considered "uncharacteristic" of them. Friends of mine have suggested that such behavior is possible because in a new environment people are no longer constrained by preconceived notions of who they are or should be. If no one they know is in this environment, then no one can spread rumors about what they did to their family, friends, neighbors, or colleagues. Others suggest that the new environment's values affect people, a "when in Rome, do as the Romans do." Regardless of the reason, embrace it. Allow yourself the freedom to try new things and realize that others will be more likely to want to join you. This could mean you eat meat for the first time, go bungee jumping, have a one-night stand, or eat scorpions. Whatever it is, if you aren't hurting people, explore and find cohorts to participate in whatever wild antics you have in mind.

embracing new experiences, but when faced with the opportunity, they give me reasons why they can't or shouldn't. You, on the other hand, jumped at the opportunity; you are an extraordinary and wonderful anomaly. It doesn't happen, so when it does, you'd better go to any effort you can to enjoy it while you have the chance. Elsa, the fact is, you have it backward: I'm just a madman you met at an airport who asked you a question. You chose me. You were the one who said yes. So I ask you, why did you choose me?"

Elsa stood there, staring at me in silence. I could see her eyes starting to tear up. I don't think she knew how to deal with everything she was feeling and thinking, so she did the one thing that could sum it all up: she gave me a warm hug. Sometimes words just aren't enough. She then got in her cab and drove off.

Some of the greatest things happen at airports, and when Elsa arrived, there was a surprise waiting for her. My brother Ammon, his wife, Shana, and their daughter, Aydin, were coincidentally flying to Stockholm on a flight five minutes after hers. So when everyone landed, my family took her out for dinner, and then Elsa babysat for Aydin while my brother and his wife went out.

I have to say, of all the times I have traveled, of all the gifts I have ever gotten at duty-free, the greatest by far was Elsa.

TAKEAWAYS:

☑ After selecting the right team, picking the right location—preferably a new one—is the most important characteristic of an adventure.

☑ Routines are the enemy of excitement. Breaking up your day-to-day experience with novel activities and new places makes life memorable.

☑ Don't cause trouble in your own town or city, especially at your favorite venues. You don't want to earn a bad reputation.

☑ The farther people are from home, the more open they are to new experiences and social interaction.

☑ When you are in a new location, surrounded by unfamiliar people, you can be anyone you want, so take the opportunity to have new experiences and explore new aspects of your personality.

☑ Embrace the explorer's perspective. Let go of expectations and discover whatever there is to experience, without judgment. It will lead to a more enjoyable and interesting life.

CHAPTER 4

MISSION:

INSPIRATION FROM AN IDOL

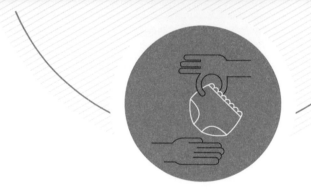

T ELL ME IF THIS SOUNDS FAMILIAR: You call your friend to figure out plans for that evening. After a moment you say something
like, "So what do you want to do tonight?" And inevitably your
friend responds with, "I don't know, what do you want to do?" You
two go back and forth for a while, mostly naming things you normally do, and finally end up selecting from a list of your usual activities (e.g.,
grabbing drinks, seeing a movie, going bowling, etc.). This has happened to me
so many times that I've lost track of these ONOs (ordinary nights out).

The problem is, if you want to have a wild night out or the trip of a lifetime,
you can't just hope that you will stumble onto something extraordinary. You

can't count on serendipity guiding your adventures, but if you are willing to put some effort in creating your experience, you don't need to.

When you look at almost every great adventure ranging from literature and movies to news reports or even your friends' stories, you will notice a clear and common thread: it had nothing to do with wealth, good looks, or resources; it had to do with a goal. Every great adventure has an underlying mission, and it isn't just any mission; it's one that is outside the person's comfort zone. It is challenging enough that pursuing it would be exciting, but not so hard that it seems impossible.

A good mission will:

- bond the team members

- drive interaction, especially during low points

- give strangers a reason to get involved and support you

- make familiar environments exciting again, since you will approach them with new perspectives

SERENDIPITY
—— IS REAL. ——
IT'S JUST VERY RARE,
SO CREATE YOUR OWN EXPERIENCES;
DON'T WAIT FOR THEM TO HAPPEN.

AUTHOR'S TIP:

Regrettably, most nights we strive for something nonspecific or ephemeral, like "having fun." It took me years to realize that having fun isn't a goal, rather it is a by-product of pursuing a goal. Fun isn't a thing we can buy at a store; it is something we create from effort and participation.

Unfortunately, it can be difficult to draw examples directly from pop culture. We will not need to get a ring to Mount Doom, fight zombies, become Jedi, or join the Avengers. These are all completely outlandish ideas set in fantasy. It also wouldn't make any sense to try and take on a drug cartel, join a fight club, or go exploring cannibal-infested islands; these things require skills that most of us don't have. So what do we do?

The answer is simple: we create a mission.

THE SCIENCE OF CREATING A MISSION

If you want to understand the importance of goal-setting and the best practices for achieving those goals, consider the research of Edwin A. Locke, the creator of goal-setting theory. The Association for Psychological Science has said that it "is perhaps the most widely respected theory in industrial-organizational psychology."[10]

So what was it that Locke discovered? Locke argued that our goals are willful objectives that guide our behavior based on our values. In that way, they are achieved for our benefit.

The two most important factors of effective goal setting are:

1. **specificity:** The more specific a goal is, the more likely you are to achieve it. A goal of running ten miles is much clearer and more achievable than a goal of running far, as there is no clear definition of far.

2. **difficulty:** There is a direct correlation between how difficult the goal is and how much effort people will put in to achieve it.[11]

10 "2005 James McKeen Catteli Fellow Award." Association for Psychological Science. www.psychological-science.org/awards/cattell/citations/locke.cfm.

11 Locke, Edwin A. "Toward a Theory of Task Motivation and Incentives." *Organizational Behavior and Human Performance.* Vol. 3, No. 2 (May 1968):157–189. www.sciencedirect.com/science/article/pii/0030507368900044.

According to Locke, "The issue of difficulty depends on the context—in lab studies, which only last an hour or less, we assign almost impossible goals to get people motivated. In field or organizational studies, we recommend assigning goals that are challenging but reachable because in real jobs people to not want to fail all the time. One way to do this is to have people try to beat their best average previous performance."

The key is to make sure people get committed while being challenged. Commitment depends on values and confidence. Some companies like GE (under [Jack] Welch) use "stretch" or impossible goals but only for the purpose of promoting creativity (thinking outside the square). There is no penalty for not making them. The required GE goals are set on the basis of what their main competitors are achieving. Thus, challenging but potentially reachable.[12]

It is important to note that Locke's research focused on organizations and employees, not adventurers exploring the world, but it is not difficult to see how his research applies to the importance of devising a good mission.

> YOU DON'T *HAVE* FUN;
>
> — YOU —
>
> CREATE FUN.
>
> THE MOMENT YOU STOP CREATING IT,
>
> IT WILL DISAPPEAR.

AUTHOR'S TIP:

12 Levy, Jon. Message to Edwin Locke. Jan. 6, 2016. E-mail.

A good mission is:

1. **Challenging enough that it is interesting.** If the objective is to get drinks, you could just walk into any bar. If the mission is to have the best cocktail at each of the top five bars in your area, that's more interesting. If the mission is to convince strangers to pay for those drinks, that can be challenging and worthy of a night out.

2. **Not so difficult that it seems impossible.** Creating the mission of walking into an airport and getting a free international flight is probably outside of the skill set of most people. Pare it down. Go to the airport and get on the first flight for under $250, and then lead a fake tour for strangers wherever you end up. Now that is in the realm of what is achievable.

3. **Something everyone on the team can support.** You don't want to pick a mission that is offensive or uninteresting to group members. If it is unappealing, they will be working against you.

4. **Something strangers can rally behind.** People will get involved and help you if you give them a reason to. This is especially true when the mission has something endearing, ridiculous, or cause-based about it. Trying to find someone for your friend to make out with is uninteresting. However, if he has never kissed someone before, that is charming. A mission to get strangers to help you feed three homeless people can be incredibly rewarding.

5. **Not dependent on success.** Completing the mission is secondary to having one. The mission is there to drive the journey forward. If you reach your goal, that's wonderful, but it can be just as exciting to fail. I have failed at far more missions than I have succeeded at, but the pursuit made the experience fun.

6. **Able to leverage perceived risk over peril.** For the most part our bodies respond similarly to perceived risk (public speaking, roller coasters, asking someone out) and real peril (BASE jumping, bullfighting, or getting into a fistfight). So rather than putting yourself in real danger, select missions that activate the same response in a safer way.

SATURDAY, APRIL 24, 2010, 3:07 PM GMT –5,

New York, New York, USA

40°43'15" N

73°59'57.5" W

Frustrated from a tough week of endless deadlines, late work hours, and a feeling that I hadn't seen friends in weeks, I wanted to let loose with a crazy night out.

Having no time to plan an urban escape or research unique social activities, I knew I had to find a way to make the night interesting—but what? As always, a great night out starts with a fun group, so that was my first priority. I invited Marvin Amberg, a good-looking German entrepreneur who sees social and physical boundaries as strong suggestions rather than actual constraints. I knew I wanted to be his friend when I heard the story of how, after losing a bet, he explored the streets of Tokyo in a tutu with a matching swan doll attached to it. Nicole rounded out our group. She was an attractive consultant with no conversational filter; everything she said ranged from entertaining to embarrassing, which frankly was still entertaining.

The three of us congregated at Marvin's place at 10 PM, excited about the night ahead. Standing in his living room, I was still preoccupied by how we could make the night more thrilling and thought about what kind of mission would catalyze fun. Taking in the eclectic knickknacks that decorated Marvin's apartment, I was distracted by his idol and sacrificial

SEEK OUT
EXTRAORDINARY PEOPLE

I can't encourage you enough to find ways to connect with people who inspire or impress you in some way. Any time I hear a story about someone participating in an outlandish and fun antic, I find a way to get in touch so we can hang out. Creating the practice of curating your community of friends will give you a life that is nothing short of incredible.

altar. Marvin had taken a statue of the human form and proclaimed it the goddess of the apartment. Every guest who entered had to pay it homage with a sacrificial offering. Coins, plastic jewelry, packets of gum, and even a pair of women's underwear adorned this altar.

A ridiculous idea popped into my head. It was completely idiotic and would undoubtedly get us in some very strange conversations, but would it be too risqué? I would wait until we were out and in the right context before I shared our mission.

We made our way through the East Village toward our first spot, a charming restaurant-bar called Café Select. I had heard murmurings about this place from friends. It had a secret, and I do love a good secret. Upon entering, Marvin and Nicole were about to take a seat. I stopped them and reminded them, "We aren't here to have another ordinary night out."

Signaling Marvin and Nicole to follow me, we entered the kitchen. They were confused and noticeably uncomfortable as we walked in between the sous chefs preparing dinner. Opening the door at the far end of the kitchen, Marvin and Nicole realized why we were there. Inside, a converted storage room served as a secret and obviously illegal bar reminiscent of a Prohibition-era speakeasy. An attractive and well-dressed crowd of hipsters were sipping cocktails and chatting among themselves. I knew I had chosen well when Nicole pulled out her phone and started snapping shots and sending them to her girlfriends.

Grabbing a table, I shared my idea: "I think we need a mission for the night, but I need you to be fully committed to it. We are going to play a game to see which of us can convince a stranger to give us his or her underwear first. But here are some rules: we can't speak to people we know or tell anyone what we need the underwear for."

Marvin grinned from ear to ear, and Nicole was giggling. I took those as signs that they were in. Without saying a word, Marvin stood up and approached a table where two attractive girls were sitting and chatting. The gauntlet had been thrown, and he wanted to be the one with all the bragging rights.

From a distance, we could tell he was charming these girls; they loved him. Unfortunately, all his charm wasn't good enough to make up for the fact that their boyfriends were coming back to the table, drinks in hand. Nicole and I laughed watching Marvin scurry back to us, his tail between his legs.

We may have underestimated how difficult this would be. It was early in the night, and people were still sober. If we were going to pull this off, charm alone wouldn't cut it. People would need to either feel emotionally invested in helping us or simply be crazy.

By now it was 11:30 PM, and as entertaining as this spot had been, we were ready for a different scene. In a small and intimate setting like this, we would never be able to complete the mission.

Our options included countless bars, clubs, and even a couple of house parties, but only some of those options would make sense considering our goal. If we went to a club, it would be so loud we couldn't talk to anyone. A house party would be tough because we needed to convince a stranger, and if someone got insulted, they would tell our friends. This meant the only real option was barhopping.

Traveling a few blocks north, we entered Puck Fair. Nicole, having learned from Marvin's mishap, took a more personal approach. She spotted a bubbly blonde girl standing by the bar and struck up a conversation. This time it was all about bonding: Nicole was going to become her best friend and then go for the prize.

Marvin and I were amazed by how quickly two women can bond. As men, we were used to building trust over hours, not minutes. It was mind-boggling.

Nicole pulled us into the conversation, and over the next thirty minutes, we laughed, shared stories, and became friends. I could see Nicole trying to find an opportune time to pop the question, and she was clearly uncomfortable. That's when you know you have a good mission: it pushes you out of your comfort zone and forces you to grow. In classic form, Nicole's filter was nonexistent. Finding no clear opening in the conversation, she turned to our new best friend and said, "We are on a mission to get a stranger's underwear. Would you give us yours?"

Marvin, the bubbly blonde, and I were all caught off guard. The awkwardness of her request was palpable. Luckily, nothing eases tension quite like laughter. Marvin started laughing at the silliness of it all, and the rest of us quickly joined in. Apparently, Nicole had done a better job bonding

OPENING CONVERSATIONS

Over the years I have heard significant debate about how to start conversations with strangers and I have found that it is generally unimportant.

I have met countless people in ways as simple as, "Hi, I'm Jon Levy," or through flattery, like "You seem like the most interesting person here—let's have a conversation and see if I'm right."

That being said, I do have a two personal favorites:

- "Excuse me, do you know this area well?" I ask for advice on where to go to see or do something. I also follow it up with a reason that will draw them into a conversation, such as "because, I am here doing research for a book," or "I am trying to show my friend around town," or "I'm on a mission to experience this city like a local," etc.

- "Would you mind taking a photo?"

EASING SOCIAL AWKWARDNESS

With enough interactions, eventually you will end up in a few awkward situations, but how do you handle them? I wish I had a perfect answer, but that's what makes it awkward: it's not socially standard.

- **Turning it into a joke:** Laughter has an intrinsic quality that dissipates awkwardness and bonds people.

- **Acknowledgment and transition:** Simply say, "Wow, that was awkward," and follow it up with a story: "It reminds me of one of the most embarrassing moments of my life..." Always have a few stories ready that you can quickly transition to.

- **Exiting:** Sometimes it will be impossible to recover. That's fine—there are plenty of other people to meet, so you can excuse yourself and move on.

- **Changing the topic:** If you simply change the topic, make sure it is something you can discuss without much thought, since you will be recovering from the dissipating awkwardness.

with this girl than expected, so much so that the blonde's next words were, "I would love to, but I'm wearing granny panties and I'm really embarrassed. I guess my mom was right: I should always leave my house in nice underwear. You never know where your day will take you."

After a little more conversation and making fun of her panties, we said our good-byes and moved on. Bar after bar, we made friends, bonded with them, and asked them for our cherished prize. It was nerve-racking, awkward, and at one point even dangerous. One girl's response to me was, "You see that very large man over there? He is a marine and my boyfriend. If he found out what you just said, he would kill you."

THE LULL

When setting forth on a mission, failure and doubt are inevitable. There are low points and moments when you lack momentum and energy and you or your teammates wonder if the goal is achievable.

- **Achieve a small win:** When you are in a slump, it is important to stack small wins to build up confidence and momentum. Start with small challenges and move your way up to continuing the mission.

- **Get an energy boost:** A fun dessert, a crazy shot, or comfort food might pep up the team, so indulge a little.

- **Take a detour:** A small break from the mission can be healthy. You don't want to obsess about it, because it was conceived for fun and growth. If it isn't providing that, take a break and come back to it later.

- **Tweak the mission:** If the mission was too ambitious or not appropriate for the culture, then tweak it. After all, it is your mission, so you get to enjoy it any way you want.

- **Remember it doesn't actually matter:** You aren't Liam Neeson trying to save your kidnapped daughter. You are an adventurer having fun and exploring the world. An actual person's life does not depend on you, so don't take yourself too seriously.

Generally, giving up on the mission won't teach you much, so stick with it a little longer and know that I'm rooting for you.

She waved at someone who, at 6-foot-5 and 250 pounds, was more beast than man. With no way to recover and now scared of being beaten, I rambled off an apology, grabbed Nicole and Marvin, and ran out as quickly as possible. Trying to get some distance from a potential assault and needing to shake off the last experience, we sought a pick-me-up, and nothing sounded more enticing than seasoned cheese fries at the Coffee Shop on Union Square.

By 3:05 AM, our mouthwatering sustenance was ordered, and Nicole was on the prowl. This time she approached a handsome man in his early thirties, wearing a button-down and jeans. She had a new strategy at play: flirt with him, chat him up, and find out what he had under those jeans. By the time our fries had arrived, the two were clearly hitting it off, deep in conversation. I use that term loosely as very few drunken conversations at 3 AM are ever as deep as they seem at the time. They often involve phases like "We should buy an island," or "It would be really funny if we…" followed by the most absurd idea you have ever had—e.g., getting married, adopting a puppy, bridge jumping, TP-ing a house, etc.

Marvin and I knew better than to interrupt the two, so we entertained ourselves by chatting up a young couple sitting next to us at the bar. After about fifteen minutes, Nicole politely expressed her great desire to find out what was between him and his Calvins. The answer was both surprising and ironic—nothing. He said, "I would gladly give you my underwear if I was wearing any." She laughed so loud we could hear her across the room. The two spoke a little longer and exchanged numbers, then Nicole rejoined us grinning from ear to ear.

The time was approaching 3:30 AM, and I was ready to bow out. At a certain point, nothing good comes from staying out any later. It is better to exit gracefully than let the night dwindle into nothing. We all said goodbye, and I headed home. Could I have stayed out later and maybe completed the mission? Sure, it's possible, but that's not the point. It was never about actually getting the underwear. The mission was created so we would explore the city in a new way, expand our comfort zones, and have fun in the process.

To be honest, I never thought it would be so challenging and uncomfortable. We had failed at every turn and, in the process, embarrassed ourselves and got laughed at and even threatened. But we also came away having had hilarious experiences with complete strangers, seen places we never knew existed, and spent quality time with great friends. The mission may have been a failure, but that was unimportant because the night was a success.

THE GLORY OF FAILURE

When attempting something outlandish, insane, or thought to be impossible, there is an honor in failing. Not that you should desire failure, but when you set forth on something that most people wouldn't dare, you go forward with the understanding that you will have to redefine yourself in the pursuit of this mission. We all fail at times, but that's okay because we are pursuing things that create fun, enjoyment, and playfulness, and cause us to grow. This is a noble pursuit, even if the mission itself sounds ridiculous, and in that pursuit, there is a glory and honor in failing. So don't worry about failure; instead, focus on what you create as you explore the limits of your abilities.

TAKEAWAYS:

- ☑ Never rely on serendipity; you have to create your experience.

- ☑ Having a mission is essential to an exceptional adventure. Create one that will bond your group, engage strangers, and inspire you to push past any obstacles you may face.

- ☑ A good mission stimulates growth. If it's too easy, you will be bored; if it's too hard, you will be intimidated and won't pursue it.

- ☑ Leverage perceived risk to make missions more exciting without ever being in any real danger.

- ☑ If at some point the mission seems impossible, you haven't failed; instead, get some small wins or tweak the mission.

- ☑ The objective is to enjoy yourself, so don't take things too seriously.

CHAPTER 5

CONSTRAINTS:

A NICE NIGHT OUT

S A GEEK, THE CLOSEST I got to hanging out with a girl in my childhood was trying to save the princess in the original Super Mario Brothers video game. I spent countless hours playing alone at home, and as I did, I realized something about what makes life exciting. Let me paint a picture: imagine you are playing Super Mario Brothers and you beat it. In fact, you are so good at the game that you can beat it every time you play. Eventually the game becomes so easy and predictable you naturally get bored, but what if we added constraints? What if you were limited to only one life, had to finish it in less than ten minutes, or you had to play it as small Mario?

Each of these constraints forces you to improve your skill, be creative in the way you solve problems, and adopt a fresh perspective on the entire game.

So, what if you could only spend $5 for the night, or if you had to convince people to buy you all of your drinks? Maybe you had to let all of your decisions be made by the flip of a coin, or by asking strangers. These constraints, on a usual, ordinary night out, enliven the experience, and you're suddenly having fun doing things you've done countless times before.

If the mission we create is the goal of the adventure, the constraints are the rules we play by.

Examples of constraints:

- PEOPLE: limit who you can speak to or interact with. What if you could only interact with strangers the entire night?

- LOCATION: Restrict where you can go. What if you could only enter places you have never been before?

- FINANCIAL: Cap how much you can spend. Imagine a night were you could only spend a few dollars, but still had to complete a mission.

- TIME: Restrict the mission to a specific length of time. Much like professional sports, everything must be completed by the buzzer—this may be sunrise or the time your train leaves that evening.

- CONVERSATION: Limit what topics can be discussed and/or who can discuss them. A mission can be significantly more difficult if you can't explain to people that you are on one, for example.

The more experienced you are, the tougher the rules should be to ensure the adventure is challenging. That's exactly why I went to Nice.

THE PARADOX OF CHOICE

Realizing his jeans needed to be replaced, famed researcher and author Barry Schwartz decided to go shopping. When he entered the store, he was offered a variety of designs. The salesperson asked him: "Do you want slim fit, relaxed fit, or easy fit? Do you want button fly or zipper fly? Do you want stone-washed, acid-washed, boot cut, tapered cut, etc.?" Previously, Barry would buy jeans that only came in one style. They were incredibly uncomfortable, they didn't fit well, but after he wore them for a while, they were functional. Now he faced almost limitless options.[13]

Traditional thinking suggests that the more options we have, the freer we are, and the happier we will be, but is that true?

That day Barry left the store with the best-fitting jeans he had ever owned, but he felt worse, not better. How can it be that when we have a better end result and more choices we end up less happy?

Barry spent a significant amount of time researching this, and he discovered several factors, including:

- **paralysis:** When you have too many options, you become overwhelmed and often want to defer your decisions. Think about seeing a very large menu at a restaurant when you are hungry—it can be hard to make a decision.

- **expectations:** Since you have so many options, you

---

13 Schwartz, Barry. "The Paradox of Choice." Filmed July 2005. TED Talk, 19:37. www.ted.com/talks/barry_schwartz_on_the_paradox_of_choice?language=en#t-1036387.

expect to enjoy perfection, but nothing lives up to the expectation of perfection, so you will probably be disappointed.

- **responsibility**: Consider a scenario where you have no choice. If you are not satisfied, then the world is clearly to blame, but if you have unlimited options and you are dissatisfied, your inclination is to blame yourself.

- **missed opportunity**: When making a choice, you invariably realize that each of the many options possesses some characteristics that are appealing and others that are not. Once a selection is made, you have a point of comparison in each alternative option to show how you might have been happier. The more options you have, the more points of comparison there are and the less satisfied you are.

Barry concluded, "Some choice is better than none, but it does not follow that more choice is better than some."

What this teaches us: Having too many options will in fact make us less happy. Constraints are thereby critical for reducing the overwhelming effects of the paradox of choice. Not only will they increase satisfaction, they will also catalyze creativity and excitement within the context of an adventure.

WEDNESDAY, MAY 22, 2013, 11:03 PM, GMT +1,

Nice, France

It was a little after eleven at night, and I was wandering through the cobblestone streets of Nice in southern France, looking for anyone I could talk to. The last train had left thirteen minutes earlier, and with no place to stay, if I didn't find a kind stranger who would put me up, I would be sleeping on a park bench. As I passed the beautiful crescent doorways, I caught myself taking note of which would make the most comfortable accommodations for the night.

By normal standards, my situation looked dire. I was in a foreign country. I didn't speak the language, know anybody, or have a place to stay, and I had no way out.

What no one would guess was that I had put myself in this situation and intentionally engineered it to be as difficult as possible. For more than a decade, I have dedicated myself to creating fast and deep connections with strangers; these were the kind of connections I would need to convince someone to welcome me into his or her home and give me a place to stay. That night, I was putting my years of experience and knowledge to the test by going up against a set of constraints that were near impossible.

There's this general rule that I live by: I always put myself in exciting, often difficult situations. It forces me to get out of my comfort zone and strike up conversations with the strangers around me. On that night in Nice, I would have taken anyone who was hospitable and didn't seem like he or she would kill me in my sleep.

After wandering for twenty minutes, I began to doubt my decision. There was barely a person on the street, and the nightlife was dead. Experience taught me that if you want to find a cool place to go out at night, speak to people who work in nightlife. I walked into an empty jazz bar and found the bartender. He knew just the place: Wayne's Bar. It had live music, a late-night crowd, and cute girls. It seemed that maybe my luck was changing.

SELECTING THE RIGHT CONSTRAINTS

The objective of constraints is to make an experience more interesting and exciting. They force you to engage in new ways and push the limits of what you can accomplish. Here are a few guiding principles to selecting constraints.

- **They should seem attainable but tricky.** If you make them too hard, you will give up. If you make them too easy, you will be bored. You want them to be just at the edge of your ability.

- **Put a positive spin on the constraints you have.** If you have a constraint that is traditionally deemed negative, make it fun. In my early twenties, I had very little disposable income. When going on dates, I would sometimes say, "Let's play a game: let's see how much fun we can have with only $20." Those were some of the best dates I ever had.

- **Don't select dangerous constraints.** Actual peril is never necessary, so don't create constraints that put you or your friends in unnecessary danger. Even if you are following the flip of a coin, don't go into a dangerous area just because it says to.

- **Don't give up at the first sign of trouble.** A constraint should provide adversity; the fun is in figuring out how to grow beyond it. It is often tempting to give up if the initial response isn't positive. Stick with it a little longer and see what you learn.

- **Augment the constraints as needed.** Remember the objective of the constraint is to make the experience enjoyable. If it doesn't add value, then replace it.

After a five-minute walk, I found the hottest bar in Nice. Inside, a crowd of sweat-drenched college students screamed and danced on tables to a live cover band.

Out of the corner of my eye I spotted a tall and sexy brunette. I observed suitor after suitor approaching her and her friends with no success. I wanted to meet her, but I needed a different angle. It must have been ninety degrees in there, so I told the bartender to deliver her a bottle of water, my treat. Moments later she was smiling at me, clearly wondering who I was. After all, every guy there was trying to get her drunk, but I was the only one who assessed the situation, saw what she needed, and gave her a reason to be interested in me.

STAND OUT FOR THE RIGHT REASON

If you want to connect with people who are being approached constantly, give them a reason to come to you. Many of us focus on trying to impress others. Growing up, I fell into that trap. I would try impressing girls, but the only things I was good at were programming and video games. And, since the nerd-dating-the-head-cheerleader cliché only comes true in the movies, you could imagine how successful those conversations were in real life.

Trying to impress people is a fool's errand. Someone will always be more successful, better looking, stronger, smarter, etc. But for whatever reason, very few people focus on being interesting, and even fewer people are empathetic enough to understand another person's situation.

I was feeling hopeful. If I hit it off with my beautiful new friend, it would make one hell of a story. We started chatting, and then I realized there was one constraint I was completely unprepared for: I didn't speak a word of French, and as far as I could tell, she had no command of the English language.

The fact of the matter is that I'm not handsome enough to get by on looks alone. Don't get me wrong: I'm not hideous, but I'm also not a Calvin Klein model. I'm like most guys—somewhere in between. People need to hear and understand me to trust me. I was in the situation that every man in that bar wanted to be in: speaking to the hottest girl in the room. But I was in quicksand—the more I struggled to compensate for the language barrier, the deeper I sank into the awkwardness of the conversation. Within twenty minutes, I had gone from the cleverest guy in the room to an American drowning in the discomfort of the situation. To make matters worse, the clock was quickly winding down, and I still didn't have a viable place to stay.

ACCEPTING THE CONSEQUENCES

When you set forth on an adventure with serious constraints, you have to be willing to accept what will happen if things don't work out. It could mean you strand yourself in another city, end up sleeping on the street for a night, walk ten miles to get home, go hungry, or worse.

Few adventures go smoothly. In fact, many of my best were awful throughout. So you have to ask yourself what would be the worst-case result and would you and the people you are with be willing to deal with that? If you're not, simply pick different constraints.

The two of us parted ways, and I went off to make a plan. I spoke to person after person, but it was clear most of the crowd could neither understand my English nor hear me over the music. The couple of girls who were interested weren't exactly inspiring. Most of us would be lying if we said we were never affected by beer goggles. In the words of Katy Perry, we went "to bed with a ten and [woke] up with a two," but I was neither that drunk nor that desperate. I would rather sleep on the street. As 1:30 AM approached, my situation was looking grim. I had to come to terms with the fact that I would be sleeping on a cobblestone bed.

As a last-ditch effort, I struck up a conversation with three guys standing at the bar. They were the best-dressed guys in Wayne's (besides myself, of course). This is one of the many cues I use to judge who I think would be interesting to interact with.

The four of us were quick to become friends—if only because we were the only ones at Wayne's who spoke English. I realized this was my chance. If I could build up enough camaraderie with these guys, they would maybe let me crash on their floor. It was a long shot, but it was my last play. I had to make it work.

Relying on a classic bonding technique, I treated the group to drinks. "A round of shots for me and my new friends," I told the bartender. We all raised our glasses, and I announced, "To new friends and epic nights, let's make this night one for the history books."

And like that I was now a part of the group. The evening quickly evolved in to a pub crawl. As we explored the streets of Nice, we stopped at every open bar and shared a shot. By the fourth, we were in rare form, trying to figure out where to go next. One of the guys hailed a cab, we hopped in, he gave some indecipherable address to the driver, and twenty minutes later we had arrived.

It was too dark to tell where we were. It seemed like some residential area. We were approaching a beautiful three-story home, and I realized that in the three hours since we had met, I never asked them who they were or what they did. I discovered I was spending my evening with some of Britain's elite. Each of the boys came from a different prominent British family, ranging from titleholders and socialites to major real estate developers. We were in a château right outside of Monaco with a full-service staff, pool house, and an open kitchen for entertaining.

If travel has taught me anything, it's that you need to contribute something of value to your hosts. It was a little after 4 AM, and that meant everyone would want food, and with a beautiful kitchen like this at my disposal, I decided to create a feast fit for royalty, which was fitting since one of my new friends was a member of a royal family. By 5 AM, we had feasted and gone for a swim, and I was comfortably sleeping in my own room.

ALWAYS PROVIDE VALUE

The fact is, whether we want to admit it or not, when we go on an adventure, we are often interlopers, uninvited guests who tag along and become part of a group. It is easy to forget this since we know ourselves and how great we are, but strangers don't, and we rely on their trust and good nature.

For this reason, my policy is to always provide value. If I am not making the experience better, then I figure out how to, fast. That might be by teaching the group a fun game, sharing wild stories, or contributing financially, but whatever the situation may be, you have to find a way to provide value.

When I woke up in the morning, one of the guys gave me a ride back to town. As I boarded the train from Nice to where I was staying, I smiled to myself. I had gone toe-to-toe with a set of constraints that would have crippled most people. In the course of a few hours, I went from wandering the streets with no place to stay to having a room in what felt like a castle. Most important, I had the constraints to thank for all of it. Without them I would have gone out, chatted with a few people, and headed to a hotel, but I would have never spoken with the guys and made friendships that will last a lifetime. I would have never enjoyed a night in the lap of luxury, and I would never have known how far I could push myself. It's kind of funny: all those hours playing Super Mario Brothers prepared me more than I could have known. I had gone on a hero's journey, and at the end, with all the failures and successes, when I defeated what I thought was the last challenge, my princess was still in another castle.

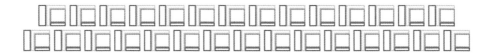

THANK YOU JON!

BUT OUR PRINCESS IS IN ANOTHER CASTLE!

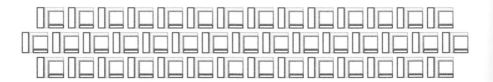

TAKEAWAYS:

- ✓ If the mission we create is the goal of the adventure, the constraints are the rules we play by.

- ✓ The right constraints will push you to the edge of your abilities and will force you to be more creative.

- ✓ To liven up your adventures, create tougher constraints on easier missions or when you're in a familiar environment.

- ✓ Work natural constraints, if present, into your adventure as fun challenges to overcome.

- ✓ If you feel restricted by your constraints, stick with them a little longer. If they are still too limiting, change them. Their goal is to enhance your experience, not to stifle it.

- ✓ Be prepared to deal with the consequences of whatever adventure you create.

- ✓ Always provide value wherever you go and to whomever you are with.

STAGE 2

PUSH BOUNDARIES

STAGE 2

"IF YOU WANT TO IMPROVE, BE CONTENT TO BE
THOUGHT FOOLISH AND STUPID."
—EPICTETUS

Every great adventurer was fundamentally changed by his or her journey. It is an intrinsic element of adventure that the experience pushes the boundaries of our comfort zone, causing us to grow. We must be willing to leave the safety of the familiar and venture beyond our social, physical, or emotional boundaries.

The gift of the adventure is not just the great stories and memories; those will fade in time replaced by greater tales and more epic accomplishments. The great gift is that the person we are at the end is distinctly different from the person who started. We carry those lessons with us as badges of honor. We become stronger, more experienced, more capable people who have a fresh perspective or understanding of the world.

In Stage I, you learned how to establish the right elements so that anything can happen:

the right people, an exciting location, a mission, and a set of constraints. It is now time for you to find out how to push past the boundaries of your comfort zone. Often, you will inspire yourself by what you can accomplish. You will take pride in your achievements. Other times things won't end so positively. You will be embarrassed or feel silly or stupid. I know the range of feelings far too well. The most important thing is that throughout all of it you are able to look yourself in the mirror at the end of the day and say, "I learned something. I am a better person now than when I woke up, or at least I am better for trying." As you go on your adventures, you will push the boundaries of your social, physical, and emotional comfort zones. Some activities will fall in multiple categories. In these cases, trying to define it is secondary to continuously pushing yourself to grow in a healthy way.

STAGE II—PUSH BOUNDARIES
GO BEYOND YOUR COMFORT ZONE

SOCIAL

Limitations set by society often passed from one
generation to another

PHYSICAL

Obstacles in reality or your perception of your physical limits

---

EMOTIONAL

Boundaries defined by your internal beliefs on how you
see the world

CHAPTER 6

SOCIAL BOUNDARIES:

MAYBE I WENT TOO FAR

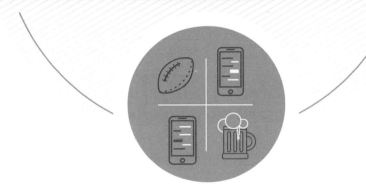

ORTIFIED AND FILLED WITH A MIXTURE of pride and embarrassment, you know the next moments will be awkward but well worth the amusing tale you will tell your friends. Experience tells you that only one thing can have you feel this rare mix of emotions; you are crossing a social boundary outside your comfort zone. Social boundaries are the unwritten rules defining "normal behavior" that hold a society in place. Often they are so ingrained in our view of the world that we forget they were made up at some point and then passed down from generation to generation.

Through my travels and interviewing friends I learned the following:

- In Istanbul, Turkey, two men walking arm in arm, promenade style, is considered a standard expression of friendship, whereas two straight men in America would never be seen walking arm in arm, because it would suggest that they are in a romantic relationship.

- The Thai consider highlighting or writing in a book, placing it on the floor, or throwing it on a table inappropriate. Books are seen as the pathway to enlightenment and should be treated as sacred, so in Thailand, my college study habits would have been judged harshly.

- In some cultures, belching at the end of a meal is considered a compliment to the chef, although in most of the Western world, it is viewed as poor table manners.

- Using one's left hand to eat in certain countries is considered disgusting because it is supposed to be used to clean oneself after using the bathroom. The right hand is designated for dining.

Since these rules are so ingrained, even the rebels among us abide by almost all of them. We would no sooner spend a day walking backward than we would intentionally throw our lunch on the floor, sit down next to it, and eat. These behaviors would be viewed as crazy, but in reality nothing is stopping you from crossing these, and other, social boundaries. You could do anything from publicly serenading someone in front of countless strangers to riding the subway in your underwear, impersonating a celebrity, or leading a fake guided tour through the streets of Prague.

But be warned: not all social boundaries were meant to be crossed. Most exist to allow a society to function. Those who cannot abide by the most critical and basic social boundaries become outcasts. If you stop showering, your scent will be off-putting to others and you will be undesirable to spend time with.

As with every part of an adventure, the positives and negatives are amplified. Crossing the boundary of standard social behavior is nerve-racking, but also incredibly exhilarating. It is amazingly freeing to feel as if the normal rules don't apply to you.

THE SPOTLIGHT EFFECT

During your college career, you agree to participate in a study involving some group-based competition. For whatever reason, before you joined the group, you had been asked to change your shirt to one that bore an embarrassing image. When you enter the room with all the other participants, you are self-conscious and concerned that everyone has noticed and is silently laughing at your awkward fashion statement. Such was the scenario in a 2000 study by Thomas Gilovich and his students at Cornell University. One student in each group was asked to wear a shirt with the image of Barry Manilow, a musician who at the time of the study would have been considered odd or embarrassing for a college student to be promoting. Researchers were not actually studying competition but were curious how self-conscious people were.

After the activity, the person dressed in the Barry Manilow t-shirt was asked what percentage of participants he or she believed noticed the image, and his or her estimate was 50 percent. When the rest of the participants were asked if they noticed the t-shirt, only 25 percent were able to recall it.[14]

In a second study, a different, more positive t-shirt was used, featuring the picture of Martin Luther King, Jr., Bob Marley, or Jerry Seinfeld. Once again, the person wearing the T-shirt estimated 50 percent of people noticed, but this time only 10 percent of the other students were able to recall it.

The conclusion is clear: people just don't pay as much attention to us as we think they do. We are all probably too self-absorbed to care. This means even if you cross social boundaries that are terrifying for you, other people probably won't notice, care, or respond. Hopefully this will give you a little more freedom to go out and have some fun and if you want to be noticed, you really have to try hard to stand out.

14 Gilovich, Thomas, Victoria Husted Medvec, and Kenneth Savitsky. "The Spotlight Effect in Social Judgment." *Journal of Personality and Social Psychology*, Vol. 78, No. 2 (2000): 211–222. www.psych.cornell.edu/sec/pubPeople/tdg1/Gilo.Medvec.Sav.pdf.

SUNDAY, JANUARY 18, 2009, 11:30 AM GMT −8,

San Francisco, California, USA

I was sitting at Hyde Out, a bi-level bar on the corner of California and Hyde in San Francisco. It was a special occasion: for the first time since college, JT, Alec, Q, and I were having a reunion. Even though we live thousands of miles from one another and it had been seven years since graduation, when we get together it's just like old times. Q's one condition for meeting up in San Francisco was that we would all watch the Eagles–Cardinals NFC Championship game at a local bar.

We grabbed some nachos and found a table on the second floor to watch the game. A few minutes after we settled in, two attractive girls took the table next to us. Knowing that JT and Alec were single, I could hear them telepathically telling me to start a conversation. For "some reason," it was my job to start talking to strangers.

Since I was a tourist in a new city, I asked them a question: "Hey, do you know where I could find a [something]?" I can't remember if it was a restaurant, ATM, or farrier (the person who puts shoes on horses). Truth be told, it was completely arbitrary. I explained our situation and, after a minute or so of conversation, I apologized for being rude and not introducing my friends. Once we were all introduced, our new friends, Andrea and Sarah, asked us to watch their things while they went down to the bar to order drinks.

As our new neighbors walked down to the bar, JT started laughing unexpectedly. Confused, Alec finally asked what we were all wondering: "What? What's so amusing?"

JT replied, "How funny would it be if we started texting them when they got back?"

I whispered the words to myself: "Started texting them?"

It made no sense; we didn't have their contact information. Looking over to their table, I realized that Andrea had left her cell phone behind.

Grabbing it off the table, my hands shook from the excitement of doing something so obviously insane. I entered my number and pressed Send. A second later my pocket was vibrating from the incoming call. I now had her number.

Leaving the phone where I found it, I looked back at the gang. They were staring at me, shocked. JT's mouth was literally open with astonishment. I had known these guys for almost a decade. They had seen me do a lot of daring things, but I had never seen them react like this.

As I sat back down, JT was laughing again. "This is going to end in one of two ways—either they will think it is funny and I'll laugh, or they will get pissed off and beat you and . . . I'll laugh. Either way it is going to be hilarious."

That's when it hit me: I passed a line I had no right to cross. As my actions in this moment suggest, I wasn't always as socially intelligent as I am now. It took me, like it takes many of us, time to learn the boundary between funny and invasive, or charming and annoying, and I still learn uncomfortable lessons on a weekly basis.

WHEN YOU ARE SCREWED, LEARN TO ENJOY IT

You will undoubtedly find yourself in situations in which people get upset at you or you make a gamble that doesn't pan out. This can be understandably uncomfortable; nobody enjoys disappointing people, getting yelled at, or discovering they are in a difficult situation. Our default reaction is likely to take it personally, but there is another option.

The first thing you need to do is distance yourself from the situation by viewing it as a researcher collecting data. Sometimes that data is exciting, and other times it involves someone yelling and screaming. A researcher is not attached to the result; he or she is just interested in the data.

Viewing reactions as a researcher also allows you to play with your responses to see what will calm people, upset them further, connect with them, or cause them to feel distant. As you learn from your experiences, you will understand how to prevent these situations from arising in the first place. This is not a justification for being a jerk, but rather a way to handle the inevitable awkward situations we may find ourselves in. My objective is never to intentionally insult or upset someone.

Now the question I had to consider was how I was going to handle this. If Andrea looked at the phone and called the number, she would hear my voicemail message. If she looked at the call log, she would see the call happened while she was grabbing a drink. This was looking grim for me.

I had two options: either do nothing and hope Andrea never noticed, or prank her and Sarah and make sure I charm them so much that they think it's funny. When given an option between doing nothing and being bold and risking embarrassment, I always go with the latter.

When Andrea and Sarah returned, I started getting paranoid that she would check her call log. Of course she wouldn't—nobody randomly does that—but considering how serious my social transgression was, I figured the best way to avoid that would be to pull them into conversation as we all watched the game.

Over the next thirty minutes we talked about family, school, sports, and, of course, if they were in relationships. Fortunately for JT and Alec, both women were single, but if I didn't pull this off in a funny way, it wouldn't matter, because they would never want to speak to us again anyway. It turned out that Andrea's mother was a huge Cardinals fan. Now with some intel in hand, I send out the first text: "Your mom must be so excited the Cardinals are doing great :)."

Andrea got the text, looked at Sarah, and asked, "Who would know my mom is an Cardinals fan and I don't have their number programmed? And where is the 917 area code from?"

She looked to us, hoping we had some insight.

All of us began to offer suggestions while trying not to crack up.

"Miami?" said Q.

"Detroit?" chimed in Alec.

"East Timor?" I suggested.

I got a text back, but I couldn't look at it so as not to raise suspicion.

She turned to Sarah. "How hungover was I this morning? My phone says I dialed this person."

Throwing gas on the flame, I poked some fun at her: "You might want to ease up on the booze, it seems to be affecting your memory."

She laughed awkwardly, clearly slightly embarrassed. Sarah was cracking up.

THE GIFT OF DISCOMFORT

The greatest opportunities for growth are a by-product of your willingness to be uncomfortable. This discomfort catalyzes ingenuity, discovery, and personal development. Without it we would be unchanged from day to day. Fearing discomfort is natural and ordinary, but you wouldn't be reading this book if you wanted an ordinary life. I encourage you to consistently put yourself in uncomfortable situations. I don't mean dangerous; I mean situations outside of your comfort zone. Begin slowly with small steps and watch your social muscle build and get stronger. You will quickly notice that the incidents that would have bothered you a short time ago are no longer noteworthy.

While everyone got back to enjoying the game, I took the opportunity to read her text: "Who is this?" As I did, I was barely holding my composure. I was simultaneously amused and ashamed of myself for messing with such a sweet and unsuspecting girl.

Needing to text her back out of sight, I offered to go downstairs and take care of people's orders. Maybe paying for her drink would assuage my guilty conscience. My next text needed to make her feel silly for not remembering me: "Very funny, Andrea, as if you don't know :P We had such a deep and meaningful conversation when we met. Maybe it meant more to me than it did to you." Not wanting to have the text coincide with my disappearance, I waited to press Send until I was back with the group delivering drinks.

DEFINE YOUR OWN BOUNDARIES

You may only be able to do this when you are planning ahead, but it is important to decide how far you are willing to go. When people are swept up in an adventure, they lack perspective. Bad ideas seem wonderful. But if you set your boundaries ahead of time, you reduce the chances of the adventure going off the rails. You don't want to wake up the next day only to realize that you crossed a social boundary that left people hurt, embarrassed, isolated, or angry. At times, things may happen regardless of what you do, since a small percentage of the population is hypersensitive. But by setting your own boundaries, you can live consistently with your values. You will have fewer regrets and more great memories.

While reading her new text out loud to Sarah, Andrea was clearly getting frustrated. "Who the hell could this be?"

At this point, JT, Alec and Q were doing their best to keep a straight face by masking their uncontrolled laughter as reactions of excitement for the game. Meanwhile, Sarah suggested what I was most concerned about: "Why don't you just call this person? If they know you, I'm sure they will answer."

Having put my phone on silent so she couldn't hear my incoming texts, I was scared I would miss her call, and she would hear my name on my voicemail message. I would have to accept the call and then hang up right away. She was relentless and tried me three or four times before giving up.

The game was coming to an end, and it was time for me to wrap up the texting as well. When the Cardinals defeated the Eagles, I messaged her again: "Congratulate your mother. I know how much this meant to her." She immediately responded, "Seriously, who is this?"

It was time to come clean, I could have just let it go, and no one would be the wiser, but I had to see this through to the end. Had I bonded with her enough that she would be amused, or would she be angry? I texted her back two words: "Look up :D"

As she read her text, I could see the confusion on her face, and when she lifted her head, I was smiling and waving at her. Looking at me, she scrunched her face as she put everything together. I couldn't tell if I was a dead man or in the clear, but all I knew was that no matter what happened, at least JT would be laughing.

I was so nervous my palms were sweating. She shook her head left to right. Sensing a scolding, I braced for the oncoming storm, but it didn't come. Instead she started laughing and passed her phone to Sarah. At that point, everyone started laughing.

Sarah was curious: "How did you pull that off?"

Now that I was in the clear, I ran her through the last hour and a half. She was impressed and found the whole experience really amusing. After chatting a little longer, we exchanged contact information for real and made plans for all of us to hang out that evening.

Growing up, I watched *Ferris Bueller's Day Off* countless times trying to learn everything I could about being a daring adventurer. At one point in the film, Ferris pretends to be a notable businessperson so he can get a reservation at a prestigious restaurant. His two friends, Cameron and Sloane, concerned about getting in trouble, try to convince him to stop pushing the host to be seated.

Sloane says, "Ferris, please. You've gone to far. We're going to get busted."

Ferris's response has been etched in my mind since the first time I saw it: "(A) You can never go too far. (B) If I'm gonna get busted, it is not gonna be by a guy like that."

I think that Ferris was partially right: Most of the time you won't get busted, and if you do, it really doesn't matter. It might be unpleasant to be kicked out of a party or a restaurant, but if you aren't doing anything illegal, the actual risks are low.

Where we disagree is "You can never go too far." Some boundaries are there for a reason. If you cross them you may upset, hurt, or alienate good people. You may not like yourself or the reputation you develop. Unfortunately, if you are like me, you can only learn how far you can go by going too far. You may cross social boundaries and learn very uncomfortable lessons. I know I have. But most of the time, when you break through the social constraints you take for granted, you will feel exhilaration, pride, and satisfaction.

TAKEAWAYS:

- ☑ You cannot have adventure without growth, so expand your comfort zone by crossing social, physical, or emotional boundaries.

- ☑ Social boundaries are ingrained rules that a society follows to keep order. There is nothing physically stopping you from crossing them.

- ☑ When crossing social boundaries, ask yourself if you can accept negatively impacting other people. If things don't go as planned, you may not be happy with yourself.

- ☑ If you cross social boundaries too often or cross highly valued boundaries, you could be alienated from a community.

- ☑ You can distance yourself from the impact of an awkward situation by viewing yourself as a researcher and the situation as an opportunity to collect data.

- ☑ The thrill of crossing a social boundary gives you the sense that you are above the rules of society.

- ☑ Learn to embrace discomfort and appreciate it as part of the growth process.

CHAPTER 7

EMOTIONAL BOUNDARIES:

EITHER BRILLIANT OR PATHETIC

WHEREAS SOCIAL BOUNDARIES ARE SET BY society at large, emotional boundaries are internal limitations held in place by our self-value, confidence, thinking, etc. Most of these boundaries are a by-product of perceived risks, situations in which you are in no physical danger but internally you process them as if you are. Think of how nervous you get when approaching someone you like or are attracted to. Your usually calm demeanor devolves into apprehension and doubt. You may have the same feelings when you think of skydiving, going on a roller coaster, bungee jumping, or eating a scorpion.

None of these situations are risky, but you fill up with so much fear you would think you could die at any moment. Amusingly, you never feel more alive than when you arrive on the other side, landing safely on the ground, swallowing the crunchy shell of the scorpion, or scheduling a date with the person you like.

Conversely, some emotionally intense situations possess actual risk. Experiencing the trauma and shock of a car accident, being threatened by someone dangerous, or engaging the enemy in a war zone are outside most people's comfort zone; they are a lot less pleasant to experience and process.

The key is to understand perceived risk and the limits of your emotional comfort zone. Emotional boundaries are not limited to fear. You could have breakthroughs in expressing and experiencing any emotion, but they may be limited by fear. It is the overcoming of fear and anxiety that gives the crossing of emotional boundaries so much satisfaction and value.

Every day, each of us has emotional struggles narrated by our inner voice. The worst part about this voice is that you think it is your friend when really it can be your worst enemy. If you had someone in your life that held you as far back, created as much doubt, and said as many awful things about you as your inner voice does, you would never talk to them. Odds are we are all more interesting, fun, capable, attractive, and appealing than our inner voice gives us credit for. So pay it no attention and embrace the excitement that awaits.

IF IT SCARES YOU
AND WON'T HURT YOU, IT IS PROBABLY
SOMETHING WORTH DOING.

As you expand your emotional comfort zone, you will discover new perspectives and new opportunities. You will feel more comfortable in your own skin, and people will feel more comfortable with you. Occasionally, you will come across something so daunting your friends will have to make sure you go through with it. If you have good friends, they will make you do it even if you will hate them for it. That's why it is so important to have the right team; they will be there to support you even through internal struggles.

THE SCIENCE OF OPTIMAL ANXIETY,
AKA PRODUCTIVE DISCOMFORT

In 1908, Robert M. Yerkes and John D. Dodson ran an experiment that evaluated the nature of growth and learning in a new way. They took a group of mice and presented them with two doorways to walk through, either black or white. Yerkes and Dodson were curious to see how quickly they could teach the mice to go into the white doorway by varying the strength of stimulus. In this case, they used small electric shocks when the mice entered the black door. [15]

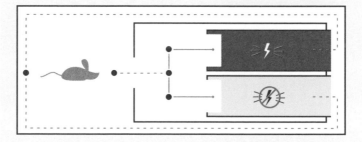

What Yerkes and Dodson discovered was fascinating: the performance of the mice increased as the stimulus increased up until a certain point, and then as the stimulus/arousal increased, performance decreased.

15 Robert M. Yerkes and John D. Dodsen. The Relation of Strength of Stimulus to Rapidity of Habit-Formation. *Journal of Comparative Neurology and Psychology*, 18, 459-482.

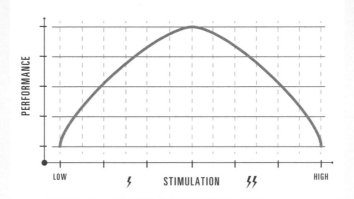

EFFECT ON PERFORMANCE THROUGH STIMULATION

Their research suggests something very logical: we perform best, not in the anxiety-free calm of our comfort zone, but in a state of what has become known as "optimal anxiety" or "productive discomfort," somewhere in between over- and under-stimulation.

Consider a situation in which you are under-stimulated at work. You have no drive to produce. You are lethargic and uninterested. Now imagine your boss just told you that you are in charge of delivering the annual divisional presentation to the corporate board of directors for the first time. You feel the adrenaline jump-starting your body, your heart is beating faster, and you are highly motivated to do a good job on this project since it is a new experience outside of your comfort zone. Now you are in a state of optimal anxiety, but if your aroused state increases on the day of the presentation, you might clam up, get tongue-tied, and do terribly. It is all about finding that happy medium of your state of optimal anxiety, that place just outside your comfort zone where things are fun and exciting but not crippling.

MONDAY, DECEMBER 31, 2007, 8:07 AM GMT −5,

Palm Beach, Florida, USA

My brain shorted out when Jordan told me what was happening. I was in shock. I had spent so much time participating in activities with perceived risk that I didn't know how to process the fact that we were in genuine danger. From what I could gather, the guy yelling at Jordan over the phone was saying that he carries a gun and was not so subtly suggesting we leave town.

Two weeks earlier, I got a call from Jordan. Knowing how much I hated New Year's in New York City, he suggested I fly down to Florida with him to meet his new girlfriend, a very pretty British girl by the name of Olivia whom he had been dating long-distance. If I came, his brother Steve would fly in from Chicago to join us. I was told everything was taken care of: Jordan would stay with his girlfriend, and her best friend Lisa would arrange accommodations for Jordan's brother and me. This sounded great, but what

IT DOESN'T HURT TO GET THE DETAILS

A lot of time in an adventure can be spent embracing the unknown. Often this means a fun, explorative experience. At times opportunities will appear that seem too good to be true, but knowing what to expect will prevent potential discomfort, especially when you are someone's guest. When someone is hosting you, it is important to know who they are and what, if anything, they expect in return.

people neglected to mention was that "arrange for accommodations" really meant that the mobster who was cheating on his wife with Lisa would kick one of his lackeys out of an apartment and let us stay there.

That little piece of information became very important when, forty-eight hours after we landed, a series of dominos began to fall that led to this less-than-pleasant phone call.

SUNDAY, DECEMBER 30, 2007, 5:33 PM GMT –5,

Palm Beach, Florida, USA

26° 42' 03.1" N

80° 02' 11.6" W

Apparently, Jordan and Olivia didn't see eye to eye on something—namely, that they should continue dating—and before his brother and I knew what was going on, they broke up.

Jordan was distraught. For some reason, he thought that, at the age of 32, he and this 24-year-old were destined for each other. To add a bit more intrigue, I should point out that he is a 6-foot-2, blond, blue-eyed doctor who graduated with honors and an undergraduate degree in engineering. When we stand next to each other, I wonder if we are from the same species. Oh, I almost forgot to mention: he and his brother were devout Christian virgins. More important, he was and still is one of my most trusted and closest friends.

Jordan's brother and I decided that the best way to recover from this debacle and cheer up Jordan would be to take him out to a local night spot. Walking into a bar, we were hopeful. An attractive crowd of singles in their mid-twenties mingled and danced to a great mix of Top 40. This was exactly what Jordan needed: some fun conversation and a little flirting to remind him he was a catch. His brother and I were quite proud of ourselves until we realized how small Palm Beach is. Olivia was standing at the bar, sharing a cocktail with a well-known male model-socialite.

When Jordan and Olivia saw each other, any progress we had made in cheering him up disappeared. Dealing with this kind of emotional growth was not what any of us had in mind for this trip, but spending our time complaining about it would get us nowhere. Coping with such a personal matter as a breakup can be very lonely process, and I had no idea how to deal with it at this point in my life.

His brother and I took Jordan to another room and tried to move on, but Olivia kept walking by, flaunting her new plaything. Clearly she wanted to hurt Jordan, so she called Lisa and complained about him being around.

Lisa decided that the best way for her to get rid of Jordan would be to text him conversational but slightly suggestive messages. This was an ingenious move because her overprotective, jealous, macho mobster boyfriend would periodically go through her phone. On seeing the texts, her boyfriend was infuriated by what he thought was Jordan's disrespectful flirting with Lisa. That evening the mobster called Jordan and "politely" suggested that he and Lisa should end their communication.

Unfortunately, Lisa didn't stop texting Jordan, which only served to aggravate the mobster even more. He was so angered by what he viewed as Jordan's continued disrespect that he cracked while leaving dinner that night. Apparently, while trying to leave the restaurant parking lot, the mobster pulled his gun out on the driver of an SUV who was taking too long to get out of his way.

A little after 8 AM the next day (New Year's Day), Jordan received a second phone call not-so-gently telling him and his friends to get out of town.

So there we were in the middle of Florida, alienated from the only people we knew and evicted from the place we were staying. Jordan was an emotional wreck, and a madman with a gun was threatening us. All we could do was get in our rental car and start driving south, hoping that we would find a solution along the way.

Sitting in silence, we sped south down I-95, taking the speed limit more as a suggestion than a law, as we tried to get as far as possible from Lisa and the mobster.

We were stressed and freaking out, we had no plan, and, worst of all, we had no idea how far the mobster would go to make our lives miserable. We had already left town, but would he come after us and try to hurt us?

EMOTIONAL PAIN
IS REAL PAIN

When you think back to the most painful experiences of your life, it's likely that you'll think of bad breakups, the passing of loved ones, or an incredibly stressful or emotionally straining period. This strikes many people as odd because you'd expect the most painful moments of our lives to involve getting sick, breaking bones, or sustaining some kind of physical injury. So why is it that, even though we've all experienced some kind of physical pain, the emotional pain stands out?

Research by Matthew D. Lieberman and Naomi I. Eisenberger discovered that sections of the anterior cingulate cortex (ACC) in our brains are involved with the processing of both physical pain and what they refer to as social pain (rejection, exclusion, ostracism)[16a]. In his book, *Social: Why Our Brains are Wired to Connect*, Lieberman explores their evidence in depth, highlighting cultural examples, brain scans, and outside research. Lieberman believes that "our brains evolved to experience threats to our social connections in much the same way they experience physical pain.... We intuitively believe social and physical pain are radically different kinds of experiences, yet the way our brains treat them suggests that they are more similar than we imagine."[16b]

It stands to reason from Eisenberger and Lieberman's research that since you can experience emotional pain with just a thought and no outside stimulus, then this kind of trauma has the potential to lasta longer than physical pain, and these memories can be much more vivid.

16a Matthew D. Lieberman and Naomi I. Eisenberger. "A pain, by any other name (rejection, exclusion, ostracism), still hurts the same: The role of dorsal anterior cingulate cortex in social and physical pain." In *Social Neuroscience: People thinking About People*, edited by John Cacioppo, Penny Visser, and Cynthia Pickett, 167-188. Cambridge, MA: MIT Press, 2006. http://www.scn.ucla.edu/pdf/SocialPainChicago.pdf.
16b Matthew D. Lieberman. *Social: Why Our Brains are Wired to Connect*. (New York: Crown, 2013), 4.

DON'T TRY TO REASON WITH CRAZY

The problem with trying to reason with someone who's crazy or in an extreme emotional state is that there is no one to reason with. Reason requires a context of rational thinking. In an extreme emotional state, people are so preoccupied with the intensity of their situation that logic doesn't apply. We have all probably been there at some point: You get so frustrated, angry, etc. that people could say the most intelligent things to you, but you can't hear them. You are too preoccupied.

When people are in one of these states, especially if you don't know them, your best move may be to stay away. I'm not saying abandon a friend; I'm saying that trying to reason with someone may not work.

The bigger problem is that when you leave the realm of rational behavior, people become less predictable, and the normal boundaries of conduct can deteriorate very quickly. Be careful.

Having had no exposure to such emotionally straining situations, I began to get more anxious by the moment, imagining all the possible dreadful outcomes. I needed a distraction, particularly after Jordan's best attempt to break the silence was to inform us that before coming to the United States, the mobster had headed up an elite Special Forces unit in some unpronounceable Eastern European country.

I searched through my phone book for any person who might be able to put us up for the night, but everyone we called was away for the holiday weekend. In short, we were screwed. My anxiety was building, my right leg was shaking uncontrollably, and even with the air conditioner on max, I was sweating through my clothes. The one thing we had going for us was that this was still better than being in New York on New Year's Eve.

THE
BEN FRANKLIN EFFECT

People have often shared with me that they don't like to ask for favors. They take pride in accomplishing everything on their own. I find this ridiculous and shortsighted. First of all, if you want to accomplish anything truly exceptional, you probably need a very strong team in place. Secondly, people love helping and contributing to one another—let them. Third, if the concern is being rejected, it is much harder to get a no than you might think. In fact, I would encourage you to go out and make requests from strangers and see how often they agree to whatever you ask. You will find yourself enjoying some unexpected rewards, all because you were willing to make a request or ask for a favor.

More importantly, research has shown that people will like you more if they do you a favor.[17] We call this the Ben Franklin effect. In his autobiography, Benjamin Franklin shares a story about an influential man that was not a fan of Franklin. Unwilling to go out of his way to win this person over, Franklin took a different strategy, and asked him a favor. Franklin believed that someone who has done you a favor is more likely to do another favor for you than someone that you have done a favor for.[18] His bet paid off and soon after asking to borrow a rare book, the two developed a relationship, which grew into a friendship until the man's passing.

Next time you need something, and even if you don't need anything, you should ask people for favors. Everyone wins—you get support, they get to contribute, they will like you more, and you will get the results of the favor.

17   Jon Jecker and David Landy. "Liking a Person as a Function of Doing Him a Favour." *Human Relations* 1969; 22; 371. http://hum.sagepub.com/content/22/4/371. extract.
18   Benjamin Franklin, *The Autobiography of Benjamin Franklin*. Page 88.

Jordan and his brother weren't doing much better. His brother's normal stoic demeanor devolved into clenching the steering wheel for dear life, knuckles turning white, trying to grasp any bit of control he could. Jordan lay in the back, occasionally cursing in that adorable Midwestern version of foul language, saying things like "Dagnabbit!" and "This is bull spit!" He would then hit something and go silent again.

After a half hour on the road, the situation looked grim. We would have to find a cheap motel in Fort Lauderdale or Miami, if there were any available. Remember, this was the era before the iPhone. We couldn't just use an app to find a place nearby; we would have to get in front of a computer with an Internet connection. Just as all hope had nearly disappeared, we saw signs for Boca Raton (a town famous for its rich, old, retired Jews), and it turned out that a family friend, Abe, just so happened to be one of these old rich Jews. Abe had managed to amass the largest chain of bodegas up and down the East Coast, which translated into more money than anyone could spend in a lifetime. If we were lucky, he would be able to host us in his McMansion.

After a five-minute call with Abe, we were driving ten miles an hour through the streets of Boca, avoiding old women with walkers and antique Ferraris. Being behind a gated community provided a sense of security; whether we were any safer was questionable, but sometimes the impression of safety is all you need.

It had been two hours since the phone call, and unsurprisingly we were all still shaken up. When you experience a shock to your system, you can't necessarily just walk it off. It takes time to process and recover. We each dealt with it differently: while Jordan wanted to lie out in the sun, his brother went for a run, and I needed to get organized.

Now that I could think for a moment, we had to triage the priorities:

1. Get far enough from the mobster to let him calm down. Hopefully the thirty or so miles we had traveled were enough. After all how would he ever find us? Especially in Boca, since no twenty-something would ever voluntarily spend their time there.

2. Find a safe place to stay. I think we were good for at least a night.

3. Calm down and relax.

4. Cheer up Jordan from his fearful and depressed state.

5. Figure out what to do for New Year's Eve.

When I am in a state of shock, I need to find a solution to the problem. Since we weren't dealing with reasonable people, nothing I came up with seemed to make sense. Realizing the futility of my endeavor, I switched my focus to cheering us up and creating a New Year's plan. After running a few searches online and reading reviews on local nightlife, I realized the options looked grim. The few local bars and restaurants seemed designed for early-bird specials and senior-citizen discounts.

WHEN UNDER EMOTIONAL STRAIN:
PROCESSING SHOCK AND FAILURE

When our emotions are pushed far past their normal boundaries, it can be difficult for us to process them. Each person reacts differently under these conditions: People will often cry, suffer from anxiety, get angry, or go quiet or stoic. It is not unheard of for people to freeze up completely. You will notice that as you push your boundaries, or as your boundaries are pushed for you, the emotions that are triggered can be overwhelming.

It can be difficult to have strong emotions, and it is critical that we learn ways to process them in a manner that is healthy for us. I want to emphasize: I am not a medical professional, and I am not qualified to give advice about this. So, if you do find that your experiences push you far outside the normal emotional range, make sure to speak to a professional.

We faced a big challenge: if we didn't want to spend our night watching reruns of *Law & Order* or *The Twilight Zone* on Abe's massive TV (which would still have been better than New Year's in New York), we would need to either go to another town or get people to come over. Since none of us wanted to be the designated driver, and taking a taxi round-trip was out of our budget, we had to invite people over. Unfortunately, we didn't know anyone to invite or, to clarify, we didn't know anyone who didn't smell like denture glue. We also had to take into account the fact that this was a Monday and New Year's Eve.

In our predicament, I fell back on every desperate person's greatest asset for answers . . . yes, the Internet. After all, the Internet has never led anyone astray, ever. I had this genius plan (words I use very loosely): I would go on a dating site, create the most amazing account ever, and then send out messages to every non-crazy-looking girl within thirty miles, telling them we were throwing a barbecue party at this mansion and they could bring their friends.

This was a bold move for many reasons—not the least of which was that if only a handful of people showed up, it would be intensely awkward. They would walk into a huge house expecting a party and instead see three guys standing in the kitchen organizing buns for toasting. I would henceforth be labeled that super creepy guy from the Internet and become the worst online-dating story of their lives. Being much more sensitive back then, I would have been mortified if this happened and would have spent the days that followed beating myself up. Also, if I spent the next six hours messaging and got nowhere, I would have no time to formulate a backup plan.

After checking in with Jordan and seeing how down he was on himself and how bad he felt for putting us in this situation, I decided to move forward with the dating site plan. Truthfully, I was just happy not to be in New York on this awful amateur holiday, but Jordan was one of my favorite people, and I would gladly risk embarrassment and emotional discomfort if there was a chance it would make him feel better.

I had my mission: get a group together and make Jordan's year end on a good note. Unfortunately, the odds of success were quickly approaching zero by the moment. We knew nobody, we were hiding out in the middle of an elderly community, we had no safe way to get around, and it was noon on New Year's Day. But this is when the champions are made. Either you turn around your experience or you give up, and I was not about to give up on Jordan.

First thing I needed to do was write a profile. I knew one important fact: I can never tell people how great I am. I have to show them so that they think and feel it for themselves. I couldn't tell girls I was fun and funny; my profile had to express it. It had to stand out and be irresistible. This was my About Me section:

"Some things you should know about me: I was part of the original team that reached the top of Everest. By the age of 12, I had won a Nobel Peace Prize for having created an agreement between the Capulets and the Montagues. I personally trained Chuck Norris. I have a body temperature of 96 degrees making me about 2 percent cooler than anyone else on earth. I have never lost at rock, paper, scissors. (My secret is to always choose rock.) I was the first person in history to divide by zero. I am the world's foremost horse whisperer. I once fought off a wild bear, saving an entire orphanage, using nothing but an eggplant, powdered milk, a D battery, and a roll of duct tape.

At the age of nine I named a soda that I invented after a physician who saved my life, Dr. David Pepper. I have no belly button. By sheer willpower alone, I make cars levitate. Every Tuesday afternoon, I volunteer as a lion tamer. I am the only American member of Menudo. I have perfect pitch, but only when I sing 17th-century Turkish hymns.

I have always found Waldo. I have achieved all this, but I have not yet found the love of my life."

I spent hours crafting email after email hoping anyone would respond. I must have sent out more than 200 messages. Then, after two hours of continuous messaging, it happened: I got my first response, and then another, and another, more than twenty in total.

I faced one small problem: how many people are available for a party on New Year's Eve when they are invited that day? Yet shockingly, after five hours of continuous messaging, two girls had confirmed, each saying she would bring a friend with her. I had mixed emotions. I was insanely proud of myself that this plan was somehow coming together, even if only to a small degree, but these numbers were far too awkward. If it were one girl and her friend I could make it a double date; instead, I had two girls coming to meet me, each of whom had a friend. It was exactly the scenario I didn't want. The seven of us in a house that big does not make for an epic barbecue party, but it does make for the setup of a bad horror film.

Sometimes the only viable option is to do your best and see how things turn out. In reality, if this night was a total train wreck, we would just feel bad, but none of us would be in any true danger. It just felt like we were because we were outside our emotional comfort zone.

At about 8:15 PM one of the girls showed up with her sister. The older of the two was clearly the person with whom I had been communicating, although she was about twenty pounds heavier in person than in her photos, and her fake tan looked like a shade of orange that nature usually reserves for poisonous bugs. Unfortunately I had no grounds to complain about being misled since even though I looked like my photo, my "epic barbecue party" wasn't exactly as advertised.

SHOW VS. TELL

Expressing our talents and who we are is a complex art. If you tell people all of your wonderful traits, it is questionable if they would believe that you actually possess them. If you are actually funny, they would laugh at your stories and writing. If you are fun, they would enjoy the time they spent with you.

If you want people to get you, express who you are through your actions and words, not by providing a resume. They will understand you are smart by the conversations you have, not by bragging about your degrees.

FIND AN EXTERNAL REASON

What motivates us can often be surprising. Left to my own devices, I might stay home rather than go to the gym and justify my slothful behavior by saying I have to send out an email or I'm too tired. It seems very easy to break agreements we make with ourselves. Part of it is that we can justify it so easily, while another part is that there is no one to hold us accountable.

If I had a friend meeting me at the gym, there is no chance I would skip out. Never wanting to leave a friend hanging functions as a great motivator. External motivators are perfect for situations in which our internal motivation won't be enough to have us follow through with our desired outcome. Knowing that you don't want to let others down, you can make commitments to your friends, family, and colleagues. If you think you need more accountability, tell as many people as you can what you intend to do. The more people who know, the less likely you are to back out and the more likely you are to follow through.

Other than the constant concern that her skin was emitting low levels of radiation, the two were relatively cute, average-height bleached blondes dressed in sports jerseys. I wondered if this was a family uniform or if they thought we were going to a football game. Welcoming them in, I was cringing with discomfort. I felt the continuous need to assure them that they were the first ones there, and more people were coming. Uneasy with my failure in creating a turnout, I asked Jordan and his brother to give them a tour of the place, as I waited for more of the guests. Less than ten minutes later, the other duo arrived.

I introduced myself, relieved by the increase in attendance and that, unlike the sisters, these new visitors would not glow if I turned off the lights. Jessica, the person I had spoken to online, was a pretty, 5-foot-8 brunette with a doctorate in psychology and a giggly personality. After the emotional strain I had experienced in the past twenty-four hours, I was concerned she could see my plan was just a Hail Mary attempt to celebrate New Year's without traveling. Her friend Brynn was a cute but small red-head who worked as a logistical coordinator at an office supplier, whatever that meant. On a good day, after several hours of stretching, she would be lucky to measure five feet. She may have been small, but her personality carried a punch. The four women, the brothers, and I all regrouped in the kitchen for snacks and drinks.

DON'T APOLOGIZE UNLESS IT IS CLEARLY AN ISSUE

When you walk into your friend's home, he apologizes for the mess. You had noticed nothing before, but now that he mentioned it, you begin to pay attention. Whereas before you would have been enamored by the art, now you are distracted by the dust, all because he turned your attention to this "mess."

Most people are far too self-centered to notice anything about you, your home, or anything else for that matter. Apologizing for something that is not a clear issue in many cases only draws more attention to it, making it an issue. Also, it demonstrates insecurities that don't necessarily make a good first impression. I'm not saying you should never apologize —that would be outlandish. Rather, apologize when there is a reason to. It is also more meaningful that way.

After a quick round of introductions, one of the sisters asked the question I dreaded most, "So how do you two know each other?"

After hours of messaging, countless conversations, and wrestling with my own emotional discomfort, that was the one question I didn't want anyone to ask.

Jessica answered, "Well, this is really random, but I met Jon today on a dating website, and he invited us over for a barbecue party, so we said why not."

I could see how surprised the orange duo was at the news that they weren't the only girls I met through online dating. The older of the two glared at me and a moment later pulled me aside to inform me in her most curt tone that she and her sister would be leaving.

I didn't bother trying to convince her otherwise; it was clear there was no way to dig myself out of the situation. More important, I had to turn my concerns to the fact that when Jessica and Brynn saw that the other girls had left, they might want to abandon the "barbecue party" as well.

Entering the kitchen, I saw the rest of the group busily preparing the barbecue. There was something wonderfully sweet about how the girls were pitching in without anybody asking for their help. I often use this as a litmus test to judge if someone contributes to a group or if they are self-centered.

If I had any hope of Jessica and Brynn staying, I would have to deal with the fact that there were no other guests coming, and the sisters had just left. This wasn't something I could just brush off. I paired myself off with Jessica to set the patio table. Before I could bring up the topic, she asked me flat-out, "What's really going on here? I thought this was going to be a big barbecue party. Brynn wanted to leave, but you guys seem cool, so I wanted to give you the benefit of the doubt."

It was clear I could be honest with her since she was looking for a reason to stay. After I told her that we got stranded in Boca and tried to rescue our New Year's plans by throwing a barbecue party for girls I met online, Jessica laughed loudly and called Brynn and the boys over to have me repeat the explanation. On hearing about my masterful plan, Brynn giggled uncontrollably. I wasn't sure if they were laughing with or at me. Jessica finally responded, "I don't know if that's absolutely brilliant, or the most pathetic thing I have ever heard."

She was right, and we all laughed both with and at me. As we did, all the tension and stress of the day melted away. For the first time since that morning, I felt like I could breathe easily. I could see why she was a psychologist; she had a wonderfully accepting demeanor about her.

Over the next four hours, we barbecued, shared stories, played board games, and, to bring in the New Year, toasted in the hot tub. When Jordan and Brynn kissed at midnight I knew he was in good shape. The girls even took it in stride when good old Abe, returning from a party, decided to join us in the water. I'm not sure if you've ever had the distinct pleasure of soaking in a warm tub with an elderly man, but I would recommend you set that privilege aside for a truly unique occasion like bringing in the New Year.

It's funny: left to my own devices, I never would have come up with such a brilliant-pathetic plan, and I definitely wouldn't have tried it, but when there is something at stake that you care about, it's amazing how far outside your comfort zone you will go. Jordan was and still is one of my best friends, and he made me realize that sometimes the pursuit of a greater purpose can be the perfect excuse to grow as a person and experience adventure.

Later I found out the real reason that Brynn agreed to stay: she was obsessed with having a crazy story of how she met her future husband. On the very off chance that she and Jordan got married, she would have a crazy story of three out-of-towners who managed to convince random women on an online dating service to celebrate New Year's Eve barbecuing in a Boca Raton McMansion, for some reason her friend Jessica thought it would be a good idea for both of them to go, and when Brynn arrived, she met the man of her dreams.

Even though Brynn and Jordan never got married, and it was incredibly uncomfortable at certain points, I'm thankful that I pushed past my comfort zone. I managed to cheer Jordan up, create a great night, make new friends, and pull off a stunt that was frankly either the most brilliant or the most pathetic thing I have ever done. Best of all, it was way better than spending New Year's in New York.

TAKEAWAYS:

- ☑ Emotional boundaries are personal limitations built on perceived risks. They are defined by our self-value, confidence, ways of thinking, etc.

- ☑ Be aware of your thought process. Even if outside influences are supporting your success, your emotions and fears may be working against it.

- ☑ If an experience scares you but won't hurt you, it is probably something worth doing.

- ☑ Understanding people's expectations prevents unnecessary drama.

- ☑ Don't try to reason with crazy.

- ☑ When under emotional strain, your body may react in unexpected ways. Don't be embarrassed if it happens to you.

- ☑ Don't hesitate to ask for favors. When people do you favors, they like you more.

- ☑ When in extreme situations, make sure you do whatever you need to in order to process the experience in a healthy way.

- ☑ External reasons can provide motivation for crossing boundaries in a way that personal reasons can't.

CHAPTER 8

PHYSICAL BOUNDARIES:

GETTING INTO A TIFF

PHYSICAL BOUNDARIES ARE VERY DIFFERENT FROM the other limits of our comfort zone. If something goes wrong while pushing social or emotional boundaries, the risk is relatively small. In the worst-case scenario, you might feel embarrassed or ashamed, or maybe you pay a small fine. But with physical boundaries you have to consider actual peril. If you are trying to run with the bulls, climb Bangkok's Ghost Tower, outdrink a friend, or wrestle a bear and something goes wrong, you could end up in the hospital or worse. Breaking through physical boundaries can be incredibly exciting and rewarding; at the same time, the choice to pursue these sorts of activities requires you to be in a mental state capable of exercising good judgment and properly assessing risk. I learned this the hard way when the bull struck me in Pamplona; since then I have been far more calculating about the risks I choose to take. Frankly, I can be a slow learner, which is made evident by the many injuries I have amassed in pursuit of adventure.

Ask yourself: How far am I willing to push myself? What physical boundaries define my limits? How far is too far? Am I sure? What if I'm wrong? Most of the time I am. Some of your greatest adventures will transform how you see your physical limits and the boundaries of your world.

When expanding your comfort zone, physical boundaries come in two forms:

- THE LIMITS OF YOUR BODY: what you have accomplished vs. what is possible
- THE LIMITS OF YOUR ENVIRONMENT: those things that stand in your way and define your surroundings

Things to consider:

STATISTICAL RISK:

How many people actually get hurt doing this?

- A high ropes course, although scary, is likely to be very safe. You are mostly dealing with perceived risk, much like skydiving. Almost no one gets hurt. In 2014, there were only 24 deaths out of an estimated 3.2 million jumps. That means if you jump, your chances of dying are 0.00075% [19]
- Conversely, summiting Mount Everest is one of the most dangerous recreational activities. Even the most experienced climbers face a high level of actual risk, with the mortality for all climbers who leave base camp hovering around 1.6 percent—or 2,222 times greater than skydiving.[20]

---

19 "United States Parachute Association>Facts/FAQs>Safety." USPA United States PArachute Association. http://www.uspa.org/facts-faqs/safety.
20 Jon Krakauer. "Death and Anger on Everest." *New Yorker*, April 21, 2014.

COMPETENCY LEVEL:

Do I have the necessary training to be able to accomplish this?

- I won't go BASE jumping (skydiving from very low heights), not because it can't be done safely, but because I simply don't have the training. It would be wildly irresponsible. I would also never free climb (rock climbing without a harness or ropes). I can't trust my skills to keep me alive more than a few feet off the ground.
- If I were to run a marathon tomorrow, I would end up in bad shape. I am not a runner, and my body is not conditioned for it. But in a worst-case scenario, I may pull, sprain, or injure something. This would be inconvenient but not life threatening, and I could also quit running along the way. I wouldn't recommend putting yourself in this situation, but there could be worse results.

CONSEQUENCES:

If everything goes wrong, what will the impact be on me, and am I willing to deal with that?

- If you get paralyzed, sustain a concussion, or shatter a bone, could you live with that?
- If you damage something in your environment, will you be willing to pay to fix it, or are you at least fast enough not to get caught?

The decision to cross physical boundaries is wholly yours. If you do, you will know yourself in new ways. You will learn your limits and come out with bragging rights, but you know that crossing physical boundaries has the potential for serious risks. No one will be able to take your successes away from you, but conversely you cannot blame anyone if something goes wrong; you chose to participate.

IT'S NOT AS BAD AS YOU THINK

Was Julius Caesar right when he said, "A coward dies a thousand times before his death"? Do you suffer more from the fear of pain than from the pain itself?

Research from Imperial College London and University College London would argue that for many, the anticipation of pain is worse than the pain itself. The researchers offered participants the option of receiving a mild electrical shock in the near future, "from seconds to around fifteen minutes," or of experiencing a more significant electrical shock immediately, thus avoiding the anticipation.[21] Although the participants were never in real danger, in many cases they opted for a greater immediate physical discomfort rather than the discomfort from anticipation or dread.

You can probably relate. For example, the idea of the pain that we associate with jumping off a high cliff into a lake or doing an obstacle course can cause a much greater stress response than any discomfort the actual experience possesses.

As you attempt to cross physical boundaries, you will have to come face-to-face with your fears. Unless you are putting yourself in actual peril, chances are the dread and anxiety that you feel in anticipation is far more uncomfortable than the harm you may experience from the activity. This research suggests that when you are attempting to do something with a high level of perceived risk, the less time you spend debating, judging, or psyching yourself out, the less anticipation you will have and the more pleasant the experience will be.

21 Giles W. Story, Ivo Vlaev, Ben Seymour, Joel Winston, Ara Darzi, and Raymond J. Dolan. "Dread and the Disvalue of Future Pain." PLOS Computational Biology 9 (11) :e1003335(_doi:10.1371/journal.pcbi.1003335).

SATURDAY, SEPTEMBER 12, 2009, 3:11 AM GMT –5,

Toronto, Ontario, Canada

I awoke shivering and in a daze, my heart pounding uncontrollably. My body ached as I tried to sit up. I had no idea where I was or what I was doing there. Nothing made sense. The sky was dark and I was lying on some stranger's front lawn. I looked around and realized there was an unconscious man a few feet away from me. Driven by an uncontrollable sense that he was a serious threat, I began to hit him, but in my weakened state, my strikes were about as dangerous as a four-year-old's slap.

Who was this person, where was I, and what was going on? The man awoke and turned around, unsure why I was hitting him. On seeing his face everything flooded back.

FRIDAY, SEPTEMBER 11, 2009, 8:22 PM GMT –5,

Toronto, Ontario, Canada

When I was twenty years old, I took a year off of school and participated in a volunteer basic training program in the Israeli military. I wanted to push my limits and see how tough I was. My unit was comprised of foreigners from more than ten countries. During those two long months, I made some of the closest friends I have, among them Zach Goelman and Adam Vinokoor, two Canadians who were not only brilliant but also insanely fun to hang out with whenever we had a rare weekend off.

So when I got a call from Zach eight years later to tell me that he was getting married in Toronto, I booked my tickets immediately. The night before the wedding, Zach and his bride-to-be gathered all the out-of-towners for a party. To my delight, Adam was there.

Adam is a good-looking, charismatic guy with a baby face so sweet that no girl could resist. He and I have a friendship such that, no matter how much time passes between our meetings, we always pick up right where we left off. Unfortunately, where we left off was eight years earlier in basic training, and at the time, we weren't known for our healthy habits. Since we were given only thirty-six hours off the base every two weeks, we would use what precious little social time we had to drink in excess and celebrate until the early morning.

WATCH OUT FOR CONTEXTUAL HABITS

There are certain habits we participate in only around specific people. These might be smoking, drinking, exercise, etc. Be careful and mindful of how you are affected by these people or in certain environments, because it can have a significant impact on the quality of your life and the experiences you have.

We wanted to celebrate our reunion in style but needed a plan. Have you ever had an idea and your first thought was, "This is going to be amazing," and then your second thought was, "This is a really bad idea that will end terribly," but for whatever reason you couldn't stop yourself? Adam and I had one of these ingenious ideas. We picked up a 750 ml bottle of vodka and a large energy drink, mixed the two, and split the concoction over the course of an hour and a half. That's right, we each drank the equivalent of about nine shots of vodka in ninety minutes. I weighed about 155 pounds and no longer had the tolerance I had had in my early twenties. There is no way I, or anyone for that matter, should have been drinking that much, then or ever!

ALCOHOL MYTHS DEBUNKED

Over the years, I have heard a lot of myths about alcohol, and none of them seemed to be based on any science.

Beer before liquor, never been sicker; liquor before beer, you're in the clear. I can understand why this idea has spread, as it is incredibly catchy and easy to remember, but there is no scientific evidence to support the claim.[22] If it were true, and it isn't, it would raise the question, what in beer would make you sicker if you drink it first? Unless the issue was the barley, the major difference is that beer has a lot more water than liquor, but hydrating more would not be likely to make you sicker. That same reasoning would suggest that drinking several diluted vodka drinks followed by several normal strength vodka drinks over the course of a night would suddenly make you sick. Doesn't it sound a little strange when you put it that way?

   Likely source: Imagine you are drinking beer (usually about 5 percent alcohol) and you fall into a steady drinking pace, and then you switch to hard liquor (usually 40 percent alcohol, or 10 to 20 percent depending on how it is mixed), and you stick to the same drinking pace. You will end up consuming much more alcohol when you are already drunk, making it much more likely that you will get sick. It is the total quantity of alcohol you consume and not the order in which you consume it that will affect you.[23]

Mixing different liquors (e.g. vodka, tequila, and rum) makes you sicker. This is essentially the same as the first myth.[24] If all spirits are essentially water, alcohol (specifically ethanol), and some plant or additive that gives them

22 Anahad O'Connor. "The Claim: Mixing Types of Alcohol Makes You Sick." *The New York Times*, February 7, 2006. http://www.nytimes.com/2006/02/07/health/07real.html.
23 Ibid.
24 Ibid.

flavoring, that would mean that the combination of the juice of the agave plant used for tequila and the juniper used for gin somehow makes you sick when you add a bit of alcohol. The combination may not taste good, but it wouldn't make you sick.[25]

Likely source: When people drink a lot of different drinks, they are probably having a wild experience, which means that they are more likely to get sick or be hungover the next day. It had nothing to do with mixing and everything to do with an inability to manage their drinking.

Red wine makes you tired. Although, as a result of fermentation,[26] red wine has small amounts of melatonin, a sleep-regulating hormone, there is no evidence it would affect us at such quantities. Alternatively, white wine can actually have far more melatonin than red.[27]

Likely source: When do most people have red wine? At the end of a long day to relax. It is not surprising that once we finally relax, we fall asleep. Also, red wine doesn't have the sugar content that mixed drinks like a rum and coke have, so people don't get the sudden sugar rush that would normally wake them up a bit.

Drinking water, eating food, having coffee, or taking a shower will sober you up. Drinking water may hydrate you, potentially reducing the symptoms of a hangover, but it will not cause you to metabolize alcohol faster. Drinking coffee can increase alertness due to the caffeine, but it will not make you sober. In fact, it may keep people awake when they are past the point they should be, leading them

25 O'Connor. "The Claim."
26 Isabel Rodrigues Naranjo, Angel Gil-Izquierdo, Ana M. Troncoso, Emma Cantos-Villar, M. Carmen Garcia-Parrilla. "Melatonin is synthesized by yeast during alcoholic fermentation in wines." *Food Chemistry*, 126, no. 4 (2011): 1608–1613. doi:10.1016/j.foodchem.2010.12.038.
27 Fernández-Mar, M.I., R. Mateos, M.c. García-Parrilla, B. Puertas, and E. Cantos-Villar. "Bioactive Compounds in Wine: Resveratrol, Hydroxytyrosol and Melatonin: A Review." *Food Chemistry*, 130, no. 4 (2012): 797–813. doi:10.1016/j.foodchem.2011.08.023.

to make poor decisions when they would otherwise have gone to sleep.[28] Eating food before or while you drink will slow down the rate at which you absorb alcohol, but once the alcohol is in your system, eating will have no effect.[29] Taking a shower may wake you up and get you clean, but it won't have an effect on how quickly you metabolize alcohol.

Once alcohol has entered your bloodstream, your body can process one standard drink (1.5 ounces of liquor, 5 ounces of wine, or 12 ounces of beer) in one[30] to two hours[31]. Over time, you can build up a tolerance, requiring you to consume more alcohol to achieve the same effects.[32]

To make matters worse, I don't drink caffeine. In fact, I have never had a cup of coffee in my life, let alone whatever this concoction was. This meant that within a few minutes, the energy drink started making me jittery. Just in case you think this is one of those stories where I come out as hero at the end, think again. You have to know your physical limits. Some of these are healthy to push, like climbing a mountain or breaking a personal running record, but when it comes to drinking, I don't think I have ever heard anyone say, "I really wish I'd drunk more last night." Drinking is something you want to ease into, not look back at and wish you hadn't done.

Mixing energy drinks and alcohol keeps you up past the point you would normally fall asleep. When you are drunk and physically drained, you should just pass out; instead, you are awake and probably making unwise choices.

In our hyper-energized state, Adam and I needed to get out on the town. Luckily, he knew about a huge party that night celebrating the Toronto

28 Danielle Gulick and Thomas J. Gould. "Effects of ethanol and caffeine on behavior in C57-BL/6 mice in the lpus-maze discriminative avoidance task." *Behavioral Neuroscience*, vol 123(6), Dec 2009, 1271-1278.

29 "Alcohol Metabolism—Alcohol Alert No. 35-1997" NIH National Institute of Alcohol Abuse and Alcoholism. January 1997. http://pubs.niaaa.nih.gov/publications/aa35.htm.

30 "Alcohol & Your Body|Brown University Health Education." Brown University Heealth Promotion. www.brown.edu/campus-life/health/services/promotion/alcohol-other-drugs-alcohol/alcohol-and-your-body.

31 "Alcohol Metabolism—Alcohol Alert No. 35 1997."

32 "Alcohol and tolerance—Alcohol Alert No. 28 1995." NIH National Institute of Alcohol Abuse and Alcoholism. April 1995. http://pubs.niaaa.nih.gov/publications/aa28.htm.

International Film Festival (TIFF). During TIFF, the city comes alive, every night filled with parties and film openings.

The plan was to try to hold our composure long enough to talk our way into the party and meet cool people. This may have been too ambitious considering that we were already slurring our speech when we said good-bye to Zach. We were now racing the clock. At the rate the alcohol was hitting our systems, chances were slim that we would be in any condition to hold a conversation by the time we arrived at the party.

The event entrance was in a state of chaos, giving us the opportunity to sneak in as security attempted to manage the hundreds of people coming in and out. This was pure luck for us, given that we were having a tough time keeping our balance. Inside, Adam and I struck up conversations with some of the beautifully dressed socialites in the crowd. Unsurprisingly, each of these exchanges lasted only three or four minutes before those we were speaking with excused themselves. The brevity of our chats may have been partially attributed to my stepping on people as I tried to maintain my equilibrium or my inability to stay focused long enough to finish my sentences.

SIT DOWN AND SHUT UP

I know it will make no difference whatsoever that I say this to you, but on the off chance that you can remember this advice I will share it: when you have been out drinking and your friends tell you to sit and be quiet, or go to bed, listen to them, and don't put up a fight. I know that you want to convince them you aren't that drunk, but you are, because unless your friends are total jerks, they won't tell you to be antisocial unless you are going to get yourself in trouble.

So say the following out loud: "I promise that if my friends tell me I should sober up quietly, or go to bed, I will listen to them and will not argue."

As the collection of awkward conversations, disgusted stares, and embarrassing stumbles accumulated, I changed my strategy to avoid human contact by hiding in a corner feeling foolish and mortified. Adam, twenty pounds heavier than I was, had an unfair advantage and managed to maintain enough self-control to hit on a cute brunette and start making out with her.

Mustering all my willpower, I interrupted the new couple and told Adam we needed to get out of there. We were in no condition to be hobnobbing with the social elite of Toronto. Taking some time to sober up, regroup, and eat some nachos at a local dive, we felt like new men. Somehow, while at the register paying our bill, Adam struck up a conversation with a local student, and in a matter of seconds, he was making out with her. At this point I was sober enough to be impressed by his mesmerizing charm. While he got to know his new friend, I sat contemplating my bad choices. I felt like a fool. What could have been a really fun night with a close friend I hadn't seen in years was ruined. With Zach's wedding the next day and an obligation to be presentable, it was time to call it a night.

After saying goodbye to his most recent romantic partner, we started making our way to the corner in search of a cab, until we were stopped by the sound of hypnotic dance music coming from a back alley. Curious, we weeded our way through the piles of garbage bags lined along the sides and dodged the small critters running in between them. About halfway through, we reached an impasse: a large white fence blocked us from the music. To most people this barrier would have been insurmountable; however, Adam's and my military training immediately kicked in, and without a word, Adam bent on one knee and boosted me over the fence. Then I climbed on top and pulled him over. We nailed the landing—a perfect 10, even a harsh judge would have given us a 9.9. It felt good to know something as insignificant as a nine-foot wall wasn't going to stop us.

Judging by the scene, we had landed inside an open-air club. A beautiful and well-dressed crowd chatted, danced, and popped bottles. We had found the perfect spot. This was exactly what we had been looking for all night. Now sober enough to carry on a conversation, we were excited to make new friends.

Just as we were going to introduce ourselves to the people next to us, a very large, oddly polite security person walked up to me and said:

"Excuse me, I'm sorry to bother you, but we saw you climb over the wall, and we are going to have to ask you to leave." He opened a back door and showed us out.

Unwilling to accept that we were standing outside again in the dark alley surrounded by trash bags and vermin, I told Adam: "I'm not a very prideful man, but having grown up in the nightlife of New York, I am not about to accept defeat at the hands of some second-rate bouncer. This is the only good party in town and we are going in. Follow my lead, and no matter what happens, don't stop walking."

We walked around the block to the front of the club. About fifteen people were standing to the side of the velvet ropes trying to talk their way in. Adam and I were walking at a fast pace toward the ropes. We were, in fact, walking so fast, and with such confidence and certainty, that if the bouncer didn't open the ropes for us, we would both have fallen over.

I nodded at security from a distance; I could see them struggling to open the rope before we got there. I tried to keep my composure, not believing this was actually working, and like that, we were inside.

Exploring the venue, it was clear that the best place for us to be was back in the garden area. Wanting to meet the most interesting people, I surveyed the crowd, and followed my usual approach, finding the most stylish people who were having fun. I found a gregarious crowd of well-dressed partiers and sat down next to one of them.

Soon after my arrival, the man closest to me introduced himself as Chaddie. He was a taller, better-looking Kurt Cobain. At one point in the conversation I explained that I was a consultant working at, a popular fashion website. Upon hearing this, he jumped up and insisted I meet his boyfriend Jie, a local celebrity hairstylist. Jie had a personality so large I am surprised the rest of us could fit in the garden. He was dressed head to toe in gorgeous designer clothing and spoke with a thick French-Lebanese accent.

"Bubie, I am so happy we are meeting, I am Jie. If you are a friend of Chaddie's, Jie will take care of you." He sat me on the other side of the couch, grabbed two girls, sat one on each of my legs, and then snapped for someone to bring me a drink. This guy only spoke about himself in the third person, which I would expect to find tacky, but Jie was so generous and charismatic it seemed only appropriate. He was essentially an exaggerated Hollywood-film version of himself.

In the meantime, Adam had disappeared, and I was not about to push these two beautiful women off me to go and find him. Eventually I saw him out of the corner of my eye, making out with yet another girl. The guy was unstoppable. He took a break for air, and he joined the table, meeting Jie's entourage.

Over the next two hours, any progress Adam and I made to sober up was quickly reversed. Jie was playing the social butterfly every so often, stopping by to say things like "Bubie, who loves you?" and "Darling, you are so handsome, I may have to keep you." At 2 AM, the club was closing down, and Chaddie and Jie were ready to call it a night, but Adam and I had a different plan. As we parted ways, Jie invited us to join him while we were in town, and Chaddie laughed, "Jonny, you are crazy? You should get some rest. We have all of TIFF ahead of us." But like Icarus, we didn't head the warning. If I hadn't said it before, I'm going to emphasize it now: nothing good happens after 2 AM, except for the most epic experiences of your life.

So there we were, two drunk tourists, standing on an abandoned street corner, in search of a rumored after-hours party in some unknown part of Toronto two miles away. With no cab in sight, we decided to walk.

And walk we did (though truth be told, it was more of a stumble), and while doing so we recounted stories from basic training and sang classic '90s hip-hop. By 2:30 AM, it became clear that we had gotten lost in a residential area, nowhere near the location of the after-hours party. We were exhausted, needed to sober up, and were in no condition to make intelligent decisions.

That's when a flash of genius hit us: if we were tired and had trained to sleep in the wilderness, then a stranger's front yard would be the perfect place to get some rest. After all, the people who lived there would *never* question why two adult men were on their lawn in the morning. The lawn wasn't being used at the time, so it really would have been a crime not to. We would be doing a public service, helping them get more use out of their investment.

As if not a day had passed since basic training, Adam and I lay on the cold hard ground and went to sleep. It must have been the drop in temperature that woke me dazed and confused, and that's when I began hitting Adam.

On realizing what was going on, we wandered until we found a nearby highway and eventually flagged down a cab. When we arrived at the apartment where we were staying, Devi, our hostess, opened the door. She was in shock and understandably concerned for us. "What happened to you? Are you guys okay?"

I think we muttered something about vodka, wall climbing, Jie, and sleeping on a lawn before we passed out from exhaustion. There is a tradition Zach, Adam, and I learned about in the military called the warriors' sleep. When a unit gets back from a tough mission, they are rewarded with the privilege of sleeping until they are fully rested. That night Adam and I went face-to-face with our physical limits; we had been beaten up along the way but never fully defeated. Although the next day I would have to reexamine my choices, that night we had earned the warriors' sleep.

IF I HAVEN'T EMPHASIZED THIS ENOUGH

Nothing good happens after 2 AM, except for the most EPIC experiences of your life. If you aren't going to make it epic, when it hits 2 AM just go home, because after that hour we make the worst possible choices.

TAKEAWAYS:

- ☑ Expand your physical boundaries by pushing the limits of your body or your physical environment.

- ☑ Crossing physical boundaries can possess peril. Before you attempt to cross one, you should consider your chances of injury, your competency level, and what the consequences of failure could be.

- ☑ Your behavior changes dramatically depending on the situation or the people you are with. Make sure that if it does, you like the person you become and that you are not adopting bad habits.

☑ Some boundaries we cross fall into more than one category—social, physical, and/or emotional. Categorizing them is less important than your personal growth and satisfaction in life.

☑ Remember: nothing good happens after 2 AM, except for the most EPIC experiences of your life. If it isn't going to be epic, just go home.

C

CONTINUE

E

ESTABLISH

P

PUSH BOUNDARIES

STAGE 3

INCREASE

STAGE 3

"TURN DOWN FOR WHAT."
BY LIL JON

You have just crossed a social, physical, or emotional boundary; you now need to consider how you are going to get the most enjoyment from the environment you are in before moving on. Some locations and activities are already so overwhelming that you don't need to put in more thought or effort. Going cliff-diving for the first time can be enough of a nerve-racking experience that any additional novelty might push you too far.

Meanwhile, going to a restaurant or on a hike with your family or grabbing drinks with friends are activities that lend themselves to exploring fun and novel ways to increase your overall enjoyment.

Although there are truly limitless methods to engage people and increase the enjoyment from an experience, these techniques almost all fall into one of the following actions: challenge, surprise, amuse, and intrigue. These four actions cause people to engage with one another; get excited; bond; laugh; and feel special, inspired, and curious. Understanding each of these will allow you to make anyplace you are more fun and exciting.

Note: At times the growth will occur as part of the increase stage because of the activities, challenges, and conversations people have. The reason that the push boundaries stage should be viewed on its own is that an adventure cannot happen without growth, so it is important to orient yourself with that in mind. Also, just because you have participated in something that pushed you outside of your comfort zone does not mean you have maximized the value and enjoyment from the environment you are in.

STAGE III—INCREASE
MAXIMIZE THE EXPERIENTIAL VALUE OF THE ENVIRONMENT YOU ARE IN

CHALLENGE

Friendly competition creates an engaged and playful atmosphere that can drive bonding and personal growth.

SURPRISE

Having the unexpected delight of a surprise makes people feel special and highlights the experience in their memory. It becomes an anchor that they share and brag about.

AMUSE

The ability to entertain people effectively bonds the group and sets the tone for the experience.

INTRIGUE

Leveraging people's curiosity draws them in and captivates their attention.

CHAPTER 9

CHALLENGE:

WHAT WE LACKED IN STILES WE MORE THAN MADE UP FOR . . .

N MY TEENAGE YEARS, THE BOYS in my class would participate in challenges. Everything from push-up competitions to calling up girls (texting didn't exist back then) was fair game. There was something primal about it, like competing in a rite of passage. They were fun, harmless, and exciting ways to bond, earn respect, and do the things we needed an excuse to do. This may sound strange, but I miss it.

It seems people often need a reason or justification to do something silly or potentially embarrassing, and challenges provide that excuse. There isn't any reason to accept a challenge other than to make life more interesting.

Challenges function to elevate the excitement, interaction, and bonding among the participants. In general, the higher the stakes, the more exciting it will be, but also the more disappointing if the participants fail. Be careful not to make the stakes too high or you could be faced with a disappointed group of people. It is important to remember that regardless of whether you succeed, you can easily create another challenge. There is always another option, activity, or task that can be proposed. When considering challenges, they will likely fall in to one of three categories:

- THE DARE: An individual or several members of the group must complete a task.

- THE GAME: A competition between two or more participants to see who can complete a task faster or with greater frequency.

- THE BET: A dare, game, or prediction in which the loser must either give something of value or perform an act of some kind. The benefit of performing an act is that you get two activities out of the challenge, so it drives further engagement.

Three characteristics define a good challenge:

- CLARITY: There can be no confusion over the desired outcome. A person either succeeded or failed, but nothing in between. You either got the person's phone number or you didn't, you scored more points, ate more hot dogs, ran more miles, or hit a ball farther.

- TIME LIMIT: The challenge must be completed by a specific time.

- THRESHOLD OF SKILL: A challenge needs to feel like it is at the limit of your ability. If it is too grandiose, it will seem impossible, and too easy will be boring. This sounds similar to the rules of a mission except a mission guides your whole adventure; a challenge guides a few minutes of an activity at a specific place.

TUESDAY, APRIL 8, 2008, 8:34 PM GMT –5,

New York, New York, USA

40°44'08.3" N

74°00'24.1" W

While getting ready to go out, I get a call from Jordan asking for a favor. His friend Bill, half of a pair of male-model twins, was in town visiting and Jordan wanted me to take them for a night on the town.

There is a popular gastropub in the West Village called The Spotted Pig. It is known for microbrews, hamburgers, and a celebrity clientele. About a third of the time I step foot in there, I have an experience I brag about for months, and this time was no exception.

Upon entering, the three of us headed up to the second floor to grab a few beers. Looking around to see if any of my friends were there, I realized the actress Julia Stiles (*10 Things I Hate About You, Save the Last Dance,* etc.) was sitting at a far table with a friend. When I pointed this out to Jordan, he began to grin.

Having lived with Jordan for a couple of years at this point, I knew that grin could only mean one thing: the night was about to get a lot more interesting, and I might not like what was about to happen next.

"Jonny," Jordan said in his Midwestern accent, "I challenge you to meet Julia and introduce me and Bill."

In that moment, a collection of thoughts and emotions flooded in, not the least of which were that there was no direct path to get to her, let alone get to her in a nonchalant way. In fact, every angle of approach was about as "chalant" as one could imagine. She was at the least accessible table in the entire restaurant, meaning I was probably going to embarass myself in the process, but that didn't matter. What mattered was figuring this out because it would inevitably make the night more exciting.

"Challenge accepted!" I shouted to him and Bill. "Order us a snack and let me think." I was starting to get nervous. I may have gotten myself in over my head. I thought through three or four scenarios, everything from sending drinks over to pretending I left something there earlier, but all of them seemed awkward and obvious.

THE WINNER EFFECT

In his book, *The Hour Between Dog and Wolf*, John Coates explores the influence of hormones on Wall Street traders' thinking. While discussing the effects of testosterone on decision making, he shares a fascinating theory known as "the winner effect," which suggests that animals participating in competition will fill with testosterone leading to increased aggression, confidence, appetite for risk, etc. Once the competition is over, the loser's testosterone will drop, and the winner's testosterone will increase due to the success. This boost in testosterone gives the winner an edge for the next round of competition. Additionally, with every success, the winner's brain will flood with dopamine, the reward neurotransmitter.

The cycle will continue win after win, leading not only to greater levels of testosterone, but riskier behavior and overconfidence. According to Coates, in nature, the winner effect can eventually lead animals to start more fights and spend more time in the open, which raises mortality rates.[33]

This theory has been supported by research done at the University of Missouri focused on video game competition. Jonathan Oxford, Davidé Ponzi, and David C. Geary wanted to examine the testosterone levels of teams in competition and then of the team members competing against one another.

The researchers formed fourteen teams, each comprised of three male strangers, and had the teams go head-to-head, playing Unreal Tournament 2004, a first-person-shooter video game (each team member plays a character with a gun who must kill members of the competing team). The newly formed teams were given six hours to practice together and had their testosterone levels tested twice before competition began and twice after.

33 John Coates. *The Hour Between Dog and Wolf,* 27.

Members of the winning team with the highest scores had an immediate increase in testosterone after game play, but when the team members competed against one another, the higher-ranking men had lower testosterone levels afterward. The study suggests that when we compete against strangers or enemies and win, we feel rewarded, but when we defeat those we are familiar with or close to, we don't have the same testosterone rush and this we don't gloat and potentially alienate our allies. After all, no one likes a backstabber, and we wouldn't expect great satisfaction in defeating those we just relied on to succeed.[34]

This provides three very important lessons:

1. If you are lacking confidence and need a boost, get a few successes in and let the winner effect kick in.

2. If you are experiencing very big wins, it may be a good idea to reevaluate the next risks you take, because you may be overconfident from the effect of higher levels of testosterone.

3. When competing with friends, it is best to compete together rather than against one another because you may win the game but potentially alienate friends.

Considering all of the obstacles between us, the direct approach would be out of the question. I wasn't going to walk up to her, interrupt her dinner, stand above her as I introduced myself, and pull her over to meet Jordan and Bill. That would be insanely rude. I needed to find a way to get near her, at the same height and eye level, so that a conversation would seem natural, and then find a reason to introduce myself.

To be at eye level near her, I would need to get invited to sit at one of the tables next to her. This plan was already getting complicated. It was going

---

34 Jonathan Oxford, Davidé Ponzi, and David C. Geary. "Hormonal responses differ when playing violent video games against an ingroup and outgroup." *Evolution and Human Behavior*, 31, no. 3 (2010): 201–209. www. ehbonline.org/article/S1090-5138(09)00067-1/abstract.

to require five or six stages, and the more stages involved, the more could go wrong. None of that mattered; I was locked in. I accepted the challenge, so it was on my honor to make it happen. The best plan I could come up with was:

1. approach a neighboring table;

2. get invited to sit at a seat that faced away from her;

3. find an excuse to interact with her table;

4. engage in conversation and charm her;

5. introduce her to Jordan and Bill;

6. be the best man at her and Jordan's wedding, sharing the story of how they met.

Truth be told, one of those stages was a little unrealistic: I probably wasn't going get invited to sit at a table. I tend to invite myself, but I would cross that bridge when I came to it.

THE THINGS THAT SCARE YOU

If you are feeling nervous, good. If you are getting butterflies in your stomach, I'm proud of you. You have a good challenge that is worth spending your time on. If your heart rate doesn't increase, then the challenge is too easy. If you want to live an interesting life, you should accept challenges you don't know how to complete. That is where the magic happens. You will surprise yourself. And if you fail, it doesn't matter; you simply create a new challenge.

THE BASICS OF
MEETING CELEBRITIES

1. Treat them like human beings. The biggest mistake I see most people make is treating them like zoo animals or public property. This includes:

   a. taking photos from a distance like one would a lion while on safari.

   b. fawning over them like they saved the world. Remember that they are just doing their job. For some people, that's running fast; for others, it's playing a character on TV.

   c. interrupting during obviously personal time (e.g., meals, dates, phone calls).

2. Talk to them about normal, interesting things,

   a. Don't talk about the show or the sport. That's what they talk to everyone about. Give them a break.

   b. Don't comment on how they look, especially if it's different than how they appear on screen.

   c. Talk to them about what you know that is interesting. Not what you find interesting, what others find interesting. Use curiosity to pull them into conversations.

3. Always ask permission to do whatever you want, and understand when they say no. Celebrities love their fans more than any other professional group I know of, but they are overworked, worn out, and overexposed, with no privacy. On the off chance they are not able to talk to you or pose for a photo, it isn't personal.

Surveying the area, I realized that the large table on the right was made up of six women. Grabbing Bill as a wingman, I told him to play along. Let's face facts: I'm no Quasimodo, but I don't hold a candle to a guy like Bill; he is a genetic abnormality of superior good looks. If I was going to go in for a conversation with a group of women, I wanted to have some hot meat to dangle in front of them.

As we approached, I still had no idea what I was going to say to them. Trying to kill time while I thought of something, I apologized for interrupting their evening. Perhaps my energy was wasted, as I was relatively sure that upon seeing Bill next to me, they didn't hear a word I said anyway.

I asked if they knew the area well. They were curious what we were looking for (or said another way, what Bill was looking for, and was he single). I explained that I had to show Bill around while he was in town for a modeling gig with his twin brother. I wanted them to be enthralled with him.

BUILD UP YOUR PEOPLE

As competitive as I like to be, I don't ever talk poorly about my friends. This is especially important when meeting strangers. The theory is simple: if I brag on my friend's behalf, people will think he or she is extraordinary. Then when my friend brags about me, I am about a hundred times more impressive since it is coming from such an impressive source.

Conversely, if I speak ill of a friend, and then my friend speaks well of me, the information is coming from an untrusted source.

More importantly, I wanted Bill to be the focus of attention so that I could look for an opening. Needing to get closer to where Julia was sitting, I went around to the left side and chatted up the far end of the table. My back was now facing the two other tables.

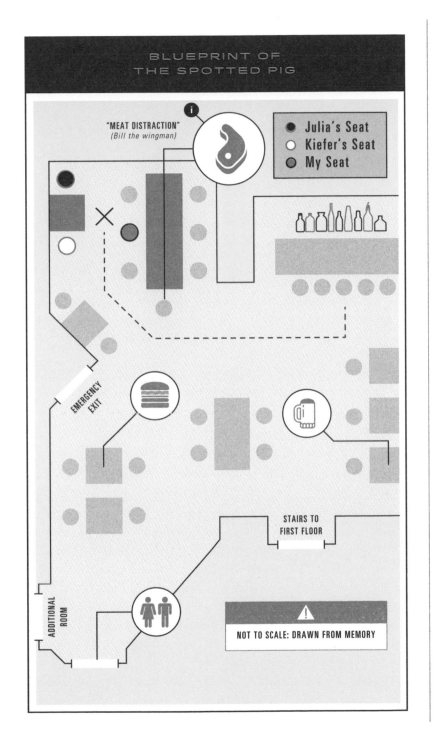

BLUEPRINT OF
THE SPOTTED PIG

"MEAT DISTRACTION"
(Bill the wingman)

- Julia's Seat
○ Kiefer's Seat
- My Seat

EMERGENCY EXIT

STAIRS TO
FIRST FLOOR

ADDITIONAL
ROOM

NOT TO SCALE: DRAWN FROM MEMORY

THE CHALLENGE FLYWHEEL—
WHAT TO DO WHEN A GROUP IS UNMOTIVATED OR DOWN

When trying to increase an experience, it is important to be aware of group energy and momentum. This is most important when energy is low, since an unmotivated group probably won't have much fun. You first need to build the group up, and this is where the challenge flywheel comes into play. If you keep adding energy to a flywheel, it will keep spinning. Even if you only add a small amount of energy each time, as long as you keep adding more, the wheel will accelerate. Eventually it will have enough momentum that even with friction, it will keep spinning on its own.

Similarly, when a group's energy and confidence is low, you need to add energy to the group bit by bit and build it up. You begin with a small challenge, something that can be accomplished without much effort. The boost in energy from a success will allow you to be able to put forward a slightly tougher challenge. As you stack successes and challenges, your momentum will build up such that even if you hit a bump in the road the group will be unfazed.

The girls were incredibly welcoming. Apparently they were in from New Jersey for a girls' night on the town. After about five to ten minutes of chatting, one of the girls stood up to go to the bathroom. Grasping the opportunity to get more comfortable, I took her seat. I was now in a perfect position to lean back and speak to Julia, but I needed a good reason to engage her. The two girls I was talking to quickly caught on to what I was doing. I guess I was more "chalant" than I thought. Judging by how often their eyes darted at the nearby table, they were just as eager to meet her as I was not to lose this challenge. Don't get me wrong: it would have been nice to meet her, but I didn't expect us to become best friends or hang out.

THE POINT OF A CHALLENGE

Never lose focus on why a challenge is important. It's there to make the experience more fun and engaging and bring people together. It's a game, so don't take it too seriously. The moment you take it too seriously, you have already lost; it turns into a cause of drama rather than a form of play. When people cross the line and become too emotionally invested, it leads to anger and frustration, arguments and fights. Always remember the words of the great Elbert Hubbard: "Do not take life too seriously. You will never get out of it alive."

For me winning the challenge was much more interesting than having a meaningless five-minute chat with Julia Stiles.

At some point over the next few minutes, someone made a comment about Tiffany, the 1980s one-hit wonder. The girl to my left had no idea who she was, and so a few of us began to serenade her with "I Think We're Alone Now." I realized this was my opening: I leaned back to the table behind me, not Julia's, and asked them if they knew the song since I didn't remember the second verse. One of them joined in and then more than three quarters of the people in this alcove started singing in unison—it was like a bad episode of *Glee*. I guess people do randomly burst out into song in public, so I apologize for all the sarcastic comments about the lack of realism.

Swept up with the excitement, Julia's friend began to sing along, and that was my cue to approach Julia. Everyone was part of the festivities but her. Turning to her and leaning back, I said, "I need a quick favor. How about a photo?" She agreed, thinking I was asking for a photo with her, instead I pass her my camera. She was clearly confused, as I'm guessing no one had ever asked her to take a photo of random strangers, but she kindly obliged.

When the song ended, we all took our seats. Proud of myself for masterfully engineering the approach, I lost sight of the ultimate goal of introducing

YOU ARE TOO GOOD-LOOKING FOR THIS

I know that some people pride themselves on their fighting ability, but I have never seen anything good come from a fight. Regardless of whether I win or lose, it is nothing I am happy about. If you were to get in a fight and someone were to break your nose or give you a black eye, it would be embarrassing both socially and professionally. You are too good-looking for that, and if you do get hurt, the medical bills are insane, which is not to mention the risk of being sued, arrested, or even serving jail time.

For this reason, my attitude is to avoid a fight whenever possible.

1. Simply apologize and walk away.

2. Buy a round of drinks and talk about something else like civilized people. It's worth the price of a drink to prevent either getting hurt or hurting someone else. I can't count the number of times I have defused a fight by offering a drink.

3. If others are being belligerent, get an uninvolved third party to speak to security. You don't want this person to think you called security, as he or she might be waiting outside later.

Julia to my friends. Before I knew what was happening, she paid her bill and left. I don't think this is what Tiffany meant when she sang, "I think we're alone now," but it definitely felt that way now that Julia was gone. I was disappointed. It was like coming in second in the Olympics: you feel so close to the prize, and you keep thinking maybe if you had been just a little faster or trained just a little harder you would have won.

Luckily, the beauty of a challenge is that there is always another one whenever you want. And it seemed the next one was being seated directly behind me at Julia's old table. It was none other than *24's* Jack Bauer, Kiefer Sutherland. Kiefer stumbled in with his friend, sat down, and ordered some food and drinks. Bill, the girls, and I were deep in conversation at this point, until we heard a commotion. Kiefer spit his food out into his hand and threw it on the floor. I tossed him a napkin off my table, which he caught and use to wipe his hands. As he did, he looked at me with an intense gaze. It was a stare known all too well by those enemies of the United States who were interrogated by this great hero.

He took a few seconds as if to peer into my soul, and then he spoke: "Screw you."

"What?" I exclaimed in bewilderment. I kept looking between him and his friend, trying to understand what was going on and wondering if I had done something wrong.

Kiefer waved me over and told me to sit. I joined the table and he pointed to his friend: "Do you know who this guy is? He is one of my best friends, and he has my back no matter what."

I was confused. I still wasn't sure if I was about to be taken in by the Counter Terrorism Unit (yes, I know it isn't real) or if he wanted to start a brawl, although the slurred speech and distinct smell of whiskey were beginning to clarify things.

I started to get nervous: if we got into a fight, he would either beat me up, which would be bad, or I would end up beating up Jack Bauer, which would make me an enemy of the state. It was a no-win scenario. I knew I needed to be as non-confrontational as possible. I smiled at his friend, shook his hand, and expressed what a pleasure it was to meet him. I then thanked Kiefer for so generously inviting me to join his table. The tension quickly dissipated, as the conversation changed to my work as a consultant.

At this point Kiefer, having made the jump from defensive to generous, offered me some of his food. He did this not so much by asking me if I was hungry as by physically filling a fork with his gnocchi and shoving it into my mouth. Mind you, I wasn't expecting to sit down at the table of an internationally known celebrity and be force-fed something I had neither ordered nor wanted (and to make matters worse, it was terrible). Taking the next bite, Kiefer remembered how much he disliked it the first time around and spit it out in to his plate.

"How could you eat that?" he asked me. "It tastes awful."

I began to explain: "I wasn't expecting it and I didn't want to . . . " but before I could finish my sentence, he shoved his drink in my mouth to wash away the taste. Truth be told, it was a very kind gesture, although in his drunken state that generosity was a little misplaced. The entire situation was so unbelievable I was half expecting Ashton Kutcher to come out and tell me I was being "Punk'd."

I looked over at his friend, who seemed just as confused as I was. In some strange way I was flattered. If his friend had been completely unfazed, it would suggest Kiefer did this to everyone, but his surprise made me feel oddly special, as if he liked me more than other random people he had come in contact with. Is this what it's like to have Stockholm Syndrome?

Having made the mistake of not pulling in Bill and Jordan early enough with Julia, I called them over. They all chatted for a bit, and rather than overstay our welcome, we excused ourselves. Kiefer took this opportunity to head to the bathroom, and I spotted a girl trying to follow him in. It amazes me how people act so differently around fame.

Soon after, Kiefer and his friend headed out. It was time for Jordan, Bill, and me to say goodbye to the girls who had so generously hosted us and find our way to the next stop.

Frankly, I owe a debt of gratitude to Kiefer. If you are reading this, I have to say thank you. As oddly as our interaction may have started, you turned out to be a good-natured, generous gentleman to my friends and me. As Jack Bauer, you may have saved the day more times than anyone can count, but being Kiefer Sutherland, you saved our night. We salute you.

Challenge complete!

TAKEAWAYS:

- ☑ Use challenges to elevate the excitement, interaction, and bonding among the participants.

- ☑ Higher stakes means the potential for both greater excitement and greater disappointment.

- ☑ Challenges provide a reason or justification for people to participate in activities they normally wouldn't try.

- ☑ Challenges are best when they have a clear outcome, time limit, and are at the threshold of a participant's skill level.

- ☑ If the challenge scares you, you are doing something right.

- ☑ Don't get stuck on any one challenge. If it's not fun, change it or create a new one.

- ☑ Remember, challenges are games designed to make your adventure more fun; if you take them too seriously, you missed the point.

CHAPTER 10

SURPRISE:

THE ONE-DRINK HYPOTHESIS

Y OU COME HOME TO FIND A beautiful envelope sitting on your dining room table. Your name and the words "Open Me" are elegantly written across the front. You are curious about what this could be as you weren't expecting anything. Inside, you find round-trip tickets for you and your significant other to a city you have always wanted to visit. It was a surprise gift for being so wonderful. How does this make you feel? If you are like most of us, you feel honored, loved, excited, and joyous. You are surprised, and that is the gift of a surprise: it delights you with a new reality, one distinct from what you expected.

THE PLEASURE OF SURPRISES

What would you enjoy more—being rewarded on a consistent basis or provided a treat on a random basis? Do we enjoy consistency or surprise? This is the question a group of researchers at Emory University School of Medicine and Baylor College of Medicine, led by Gregory Berns, set out to explore with a fun experiment involving juice.

The researchers took test subjects and, while scanning their brains in an MRI, ran them through experiments that measured their responses to predictable and unpredictable rewards.

In the predictable experiment, participants received alternating squirts of water and fruit juice every ten seconds through straws that were placed in their mouths. In the unpredictable scenario, as the name would suggest, the participants received squirts in no particular order and at random intervals.[35] According to the MRI scans, participants' nucleus accumbens were more consistently active in the unpredictable experiment, and although we can't know precisely how they felt, we know from other experiments that this region is associated with positive feelings. [36]

It appears that if you want to increase enjoyment for yourself and your friends, all you need to do is create more opportunities for surprises.

---

35 Gregory S. Berns, Samuel M. McClure, Giuseppe Pagnoni, and P. Read Montague. "Predictability Modulates Human Brain Response to Reward." *The Journal of Neuroscience*, April 15, 2001, 21(8): 2793-2798

36 Berns, Gregory, Interview with Author. Phone. Atlanta, Georgia & New York, New York. 9 January 2016.

When increasing the emotional state of your adventure, surprises provide an experience of delight and fun that excites people and makes them feel special. Best of all, it can be done with little to no planning. Sending a bottle of champagne to a stranger, taking a date to an unexpected activity, or renting a hotel room for a "staycation" can all be planned in minutes. Alternatively, pulling out a guitar and impressing your friends with your beautiful voice or sharing stories that end in unexpected ways can be equally surprising.

Surprises tend to fall into one of two categories:

1. PLANNED: Something prepared ahead of time. In this case, some people know and others do not, such as an unexpected visit to your parents' house, a surprise birthday party, or an experience, such as a trip or class.

2. UNPLANNED: Something unexpected for everyone involved. You meet someone you admire at the supermarket, or the restaurant you are at has a rare dish you have wanted to try.

Of course, not all surprises are positive: getting sideswiped on your way to work is surprising but not pleasant. In these cases, your reaction to the circumstances will define your experience. Will you let them destroy your mood and adventure, or will they be interesting obstacles that force you to grow and emerge victorious?

40°46'53.9" N
73°58'24.05" W

WEDNESDAY, NOVEMBER 19, 2008, 2:28 PM GMT –5,

New York, USA

The sound of my phone vibrating against the table pulled me out of my daydream. My brother Amnon had texted me: "Meet me for a drink at my hotel in Midtown at 8 PM. I can only do one drink since I have to be up at 3 AM for a 6 AM flight." This text actually made me laugh out loud.

As an experienced adventurer, there is one phrase you can say that immediately indicates to me that you have no relationship to reality. If anyone ever tells you, "I will have only one drink and then I have to go home," you should know you are in for trouble. Aside from the lawyer from Chapter 2, I have never met someone for just one drink (and even in the lawyer's case, she stuck around for a "tour"). The moment someone says that to me, I know they want an excuse to be irresponsible but have to justify it to themselves by saying, "It's only one drink—what's the harm?"

PLAUSIBLE JUSTIFICATION

I have noticed that when people want to do something they have doubts about or that others would view as a poor or irresponsible decision, they quite frequently justify it through partial participation. Once engaged, they allow themselves to get swept up in the experience. It functions as a plausible justification.

If you want people to participate in wild activities or go out for a fun night, you don't necessarily need to get them to commit to anything beyond the next step. It doesn't need to be an epic night of drinking; it could be one drink that leads to another, and then another. It doesn't need to be a road trip around the United States; it can begin with the next town over, and then the next town after that.

Wanting to prepare him for the night ahead, I responded, "I'll meet you, but I'm telling you right now, it won't be just one drink." Assuring me I was wrong, he agreed to meet up.

And that's how the story ends. He surprised me by having only one drink and then he went to bed. That's the beauty of surprises: they come in all different forms.

Okay, that wasn't true at all. One drink quickly turned into three, which inspired us to go to The Gates, a then-popular private lounge. My brother, at this point realizing he might as well give in to the fun, surprised me by hailing a pedicab instead of a taxi. It was a treat traversing the city by something other than cab or subway. Sitting in a cart being pulled by a cyclist made us feel like we were part of the action. The poor cyclist was carrying close to five hundred pounds of human, plus the bike and cart, over a mile through the traffic of Times Square, all the way down to Twenty-fourth Street and Eighth Avenue. I was half expecting him to keel over from a heart attack.

Upon entering The Gates, we took two seats at the bar and continued our tradition of having "only one drink"—at a time, anyway. One of my favorite parts of hanging with my brother is that he is the best wingman around. Happily married now for more than twenty years, he has the most beautiful family you have ever seen (in fact, his daughter signed with Ford Models at the age of three). I let him show off family photos and brag about his younger, better-looking brother (that would be me) to the smolderingly hot bartender serving us. By the end of the conversation, he had invited her to our family Thanksgiving party, eight days later, so that I could get to know her better.

With the bartender's email address in hand, we were ready to get out of there. There was no upside to staying there longer, and only an increasing chance that I would embarrass myself. It was time to liven things up, and knowing that there was a good Wednesday-night party at Griffin, a popular nightclub in the Meatpacking District, we made our way downtown. Unfortunately we faced the not-so-small problem that we were on the wrong side of the gender ratio. We were two guys with no women, trying to get into a club, so we did the only sensible thing. No, we didn't bribe anyone. We split up. While my brother got in line, I headed out of view down the street. Standing there, I saw two people go into a closed diner. One of them looked oddly familiar, but it couldn't be who I thought it was.

THE POWER BAR

There is a special magic that happens the moment people get behind a bar: we view them as more powerful and more attractive. After all, everyone is vying for their attention, and they have all the power to serve whomever they want. Bartenders, and often waitstaff, are constantly being hit on and told the same lines and jokes. This means that if you want to connect with them for any reason, you have to stand out, and you have to know that your chances are slim to none.

But be warned: outside of the context of their work, their allure might be gone. So be careful in pursuing this group because the last thing you would want is to alienate yourself from your local bar.

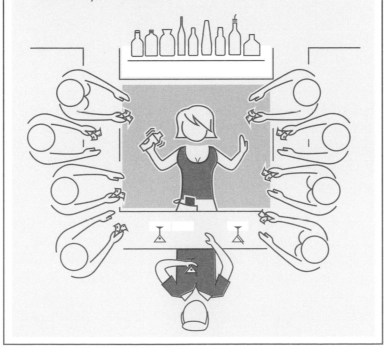

SURPRISE REACTIONS

Not everyone reacts the same way to surprises. Some people love them, while many people are uncomfortable with them. Before you surprise someone, you should make sure he or she enjoys these experiences. I have found people tend to have the following types of responses:

- **Delight:** They love surprises; they enjoy the unexpected nature and are left in a state of awe.

- **Shock:** The sudden change in an experience due to a surprise can send people into shock or, for some, a state of anxiety.

- **Anticipation:** For some, knowing that a surprise is coming but not knowing what it is can be a source of anxiety. These people enjoy an experience more when they have the opportunity to mentally prepare themselves, because then they have something to look forward to. These people enjoy the anticipation of a treat more than they like an unexpected experience.

I pulled my brother out of the line and told him to play along. We walked into the obviously closed venue and immediately an employee behind the bar said, "Sorry, we are closed." But it was too late; I was already talking to one of the people whom I had seen walk in a few minutes before.

"Kiefer, is that you? I haven't seen you since we drank together at The Spotted Pig. How have you been?"

Kiefer turned to see us and waved us in. We sat at the bar all lined up: Kiefer's friend, Kiefer, my brother, and me; at this point, my brother was grinning uncontrollably.

The bartender asked us what we wanted and I pointed at Kiefer's drink. We were each brought a whiskey neat and a bottle of Coke. Then Kiefer did something a little unexpected: he asked me if I knew how to drink whiskey. It felt like a great sensei teaching a student sacred knowledge passed down from generation to generation. Frankly, if someone was going to teach me how to drink whiskey, Kiefer was the right guy to do it.

"You will notice that if you just drink straight whiskey, it can be a little harsh, so what you do is take a sip of the whiskey and follow it up with a sip of Coke," he instructed. "The Coke soothes your tongue and throat. I was taught to drink like this years ago by one of my father's friends."

I took a moment to drink my whiskey and then my Coke, and I let the memory soak in. I was in a state of awe. I'm sure he had taught countless people, but it didn't make it any less special. In that moment, he was Jack Bauer no more; he was now Kiefer Sutherland, my drinking buddy and mentor.

The bartender suddenly interrupted this surreal moment with an announcement, "If you want to stay here after-hours you need to participate in our traditions." As he lifted something from behind the bar, my heart jumped, worried for what was to come. We were at a closed diner/bar in the heart of Meatpacking District after midnight, drinking with a celebrity. The only tradition I could think of involved ungodly amounts of drugs. I was imagining a powder-covered mirror being placed in front of me, and not knowing how to react. This was terrifying since I don't do drugs and have no desire to. But what the bartender pulled out instead was far more dangerous than coke: it was Jenga. Yes, the game of towering wood blocks, and we were an uncoordinated group of boozed-up drunks about to play the most focused game of hand-eye coordination Western culture has ever created.

Over the next three hours the battle was fierce and only grew with intensity as we kept drinking. At one point, Kiefer pulled out his Coke-bottle-thick reading glasses, and as we took turns carefully maneuvering this wood tower of danger, we talked about family and friends. We exchanged numbers and invited each other to Thanksgiving. He usually hosted people at a private restaurant on the Friday after the holiday and told us to come.

By 2 AM we had deteriorated to the point where we were trying on one another's accessories and singing songs. By 2:30 AM everything turned into a complete blur of falling blocks, photos, and incomprehensible dialogue. I'm not ashamed to say I probably used the phrase "We should buy an island" at some point, a clear sign that I should not have been going drink for drink with my new sensei. By 3 AM my brother had to pick up his bags and go to the airport. Everyone headed home, parting ways with hugs and agreeing we would celebrate Thanksgiving together.

I awoke the next morning on top of my bed wearing jeans and shoes but no shirt, clear evidence that I had had a fun night. Assembling my memories, I looked down at the pile of clothing I had managed to remove before passing out on my bed. Something sparkled in the sunlight, but what was it? Examining the artifact, I realized that in the confusion of the night before I had unintentionally stolen Kiefer's glasses.

Embarrassed and ashamed of my crime, I texted Kiefer offering to send them to him, only to later realize I had his glasses and he couldn't read the texts. I tried calling, but there was no answer. I tried his agent, but he never got back to me.

40°46′05.7″ N
73°59′05.0″ W

FRIDAY, NOVEMBER 28, 2008, 9:02 PM GMT −5,

New York, New York, USA

My family and I were having drinks at the Hudson Hotel, and we were trying to figure out what to do next. My parents said goodbye and went home, and Amnon and I decided it would be fun to stop by the Sutherland family Thanksgiving to return Kiefer's pilfered spectacles.

We called the venue to make sure the Sutherlands were there, and then, with his glasses safely in my coat pocket, my brother, Amnon and his wife, Shana, and my date and I headed to the restaurant. Entering the secret room of this eatery, we were clearly unexpected guests. Kiefer, dressed in a beautiful black suit and more put together than I had ever seen him, stood up to greet us. Looking us over, he clearly didn't recognize us and was obviously skeptical. Sensing the building awkwardness, I passed him his glasses and said, "Thank you so much for inviting us to join you and your family for Thanksgiving. It was a ton of fun hanging out with you last week. In the confusion of our epic Jenga battle, I accidentally took your glasses."

Looking back and forth between my face and the glasses, it was clear some vague recollection of the night was coming back. He finally spoke, "I'm fortunate enough that I can afford to replace these." I couldn't get a clear read—was he hinting that we shouldn't have come or cracking a joke? He smiled, started laughing, and introduced us to his family.

There was a beautiful buffet and four or five tables with friends and family hanging out, eating food, and having drinks. After we grabbed some snacks, one of his children suggested we play a game. A group comprising my family and his gathered around the table. His daughter grabbed a box from a nearby bookshelf, and as if fate was laughing at us, we spent the next hour and a half drinking scotch and Coke and playing Jenga.

LET'S BE UNCOMFORTABLE

There are certain interactions that breed social discomfort. Maybe you have walked in somewhere you shouldn't be, maybe restaurant staff is hinting you should leave, or maybe you are catching someone in a lie. In these moments of silence, social discomfort can build. I generally like to let the awkwardness build; the more uncomfortable the other people are, the more likely things can work to your benefit. This is especially the case if awkwardness builds from catching a person, venue, management, or staff in a lie. This may not be the best strategy, but if you have a high tolerance for discomfort and know how to diffuse it when necessary, then don't fear the discomfort. You may be invited to stay for something you crashed, have your bill taken care of, etc. Think of it as a game of chicken: whoever speaks first loses.

Life is full of surprises. Some of them you can plan for, like a party or gift, while others get thrown at you. How you embrace these unexpected events will define your character and your enjoyment. When my brother told me he was in town, I was tempted to stay in and work, but nothing interesting happens at home. When he hired a pedicab, it may have taken more time and cost more than a taxi, but it was a new experience. When I saw Kiefer, I could have just entered Griffin, but as they say, fate favors the bold, and we all had a fantastic evening. Most important, when Kiefer saw us crash his Thanksgiving, we caught him completely off guard, but he was a gentleman, and as a result, we all had a wonderful time and made memories that I will never forget.

TAKEAWAYS:

- ☑ Surprises are highly effective at elevating an experience. They delight and excite people and make them feel special.

- ☑ They can be done with little to no planning and often with no expense.

- ☑ How you react and embrace the unexpected will define your enjoyment.

- ☑ Reactions to surprises vary from delight to shock to anticipation. Some people do not enjoy surprises; they prefer knowing what will happen so they can look forward to it.

- ☑ When adding people to your group, you don't need them to commit to the entirety of the adventure, just to the next step.

CHAPTER 11

AMUSE:

RUSSELLING UP SOME TROUBLE

SOME PEOPLE HAVE A NATURAL INCLINATION toward amusing others. My brother Ofer is a master storyteller; when he shares stories, people are enamored. Growing up, I was the complete opposite; I had a natural inclination for boring people. I was so unpopular I had to learn how to engage people through trial and error.

Amusement is a complex aspect of increasing the emotional level of an adventure, since what entertains one person can be uninteresting or offensive to another. This is one of the reasons that picking the right team is so important; it provides greater common ground of interests.

Amusement is distinct from many of the other characteristics of an adventure in that it requires developing and honing a set of skills. I have told the same stories and jokes countless times, but each time I attempt to tell them better. I change the delivery a little to see how people react, and if it is positive, I incorporate the change. It is an art form that requires effort for mastery.

How do you amuse? I don't mean perform. I mean, do you have the ability to engage people in ways that are entertaining? Do you make people laugh, tell great stories, or do you know how to create an environment of joy? Are you a talented musician, or do you share interesting knowledge? Do you curate people around you so that the group as a whole is engaging? The options are limitless but it is important to understand how to provide this value.

I wish I could just give you a set of rules to follow, but like most skill sets, the ability to entertain takes time to develop.

- STORYTELLING: Take your most interesting experience and write it down, then edit it so that it's shorter, and edit it again. Ask yourself what you can eliminate, where you can add suspense, humor, etc. If you want practice, join Toastmasters, an organization dedicated to the art of public speaking.

- HUMOR: This skill might have a shortcut, but it needs practice nonetheless. There is a popular model for understanding humor known as the benign violation theory, which is explained later in this chapter. Learning it can accelerate your ability to make others laugh. It also wouldn't hurt to take an improv class and practice the jokes you hear until your delivery is effective.

- INTERESTING INFORMATION: Be well-read. See what articles are popular among different cultural topics (science, arts, politics, etc.). Watch documentaries on the Discovery Channel, History Channel (avoid all the stuff on ghosts), or even Animal Planet.

- MUSIC: Picking up an instrument isn't that easy, but you could become a karaoke master overnight. If you do know how to play, learn some popular songs, and bring the house down.

The key is to find something that inspires you that you would enjoy practicing and learning, because developing a skill is incredibly time-consuming and full of trial and error. But it is also amazingly gratifying to be able to hold the attention of a crowd and share any story, joke, song, or knowledge that you have mastered.

THE SCIENCE OF HUMOR

Can science make you funny? This seems counterintuitive. We often view the ability to be humorous as an innate quality, but what if there was a model for humor, the same way there is one for adventure? This was the question Dr. Peter McGraw, a professor at the University of Colorado at Boulder, and writer Joel Warner went around the world to answer in their book *The Humor Code: A Global Search for What Makes Things Funny.*

McGraw worked with an idea known as benign violation theory,[37] which proposes that humor occurs only when three conditions are met:

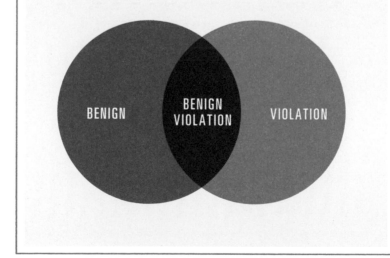

37 A. Peter McGraw and Caleb Warren. "Benign Violations: Making Immoral Behavior Funny." *Psychology Science.* 21(8):1141-1149. http://www.psychologytoday.com/files/attachments/69572/mcgrawwarren2010.pdf.

1. The situation is a violation (it disagrees with the person's perspective on how life ought to be).

2. The situation is benign.

3. Both perceptions occur simultaneously.

This may sound technical, but a few examples may serve to clarify:

- When you tickle a child, they laugh; it is a violation because it is physically threatening but benign because there is no risk of harm.

- A pun can be funny because there is a violation in the way a word is used, but it is not threatening.

- Teasing can be viewed as funny under these conditions as well, but we know from experience that when teasing goes from benign to hurtful, it is no longer funny.[38]

Because humor is highly subjective, we can see that what may be benign for some social groups would be offensive to others. A joke about a particular social, ethnic, or religious group would be viewed as benign if told within that group but would be interpreted as offensive if told by outsiders.

The beauty of this model is that it explains not only when things are funny but also when they are not. You have to find that sweet spot where the violation is benign in order for something to be funny. If it does not violate a perceived notion of how life should be, then it is uninteresting, and if it is not benign, it is offensive.

Understanding this model does not mean you will be funny, but it does accelerate the process. When your joke lands flat, it provides you a quick reference to how you can improve and keeps you attuned to not be being offensive.

38 "Benign Violation Theory." Humor Research Lab, University of Colorado. http://leeds-faculty.colorado.edu/mcgrawp/Benign_Violation_Theory.html.

SUNDAY, DECEMBER 8, 2013, SOMETIME BETWEEN 2:00 AM AND 3:00 AM GMT −5,

Miami Beach, Florida, USA

An indecipherable collection of letters appeared as I tried to use her cell phone. In the confusion of putting our clothes on and trying to find the police, I never registered the fact that these Good Samaritans were Danish.

In retrospect, you would say we had it coming. After all, it was karma, but from our perspective, we weren't breaking the law; we were just up to some harmless fun.

I tried to pinpoint the moment everything went off track. About fourteen hours earlier, I got an unexpected text from Glen: "I'm at the shore club having brunch. Get over here!"

Glen was a successful hedge-funder I had met at Sundance who, to my delight, mirrors my travel schedule but, to the dismay of my liver, inspires a hearty drinking habit.

Without hesitation I responded, "Be there in a few!"

And with those fourteen characters I should have known I was going to be in trouble.

Brunch quickly turned into an amusing mix of story swapping and cocktails. We were having so much fun that I hardly noticed that each of us was four drinks in and it was only 3 PM.

In the all-too-predictable nature of Art Basel Miami Beach, the next four hours became a blur of parties, drinks, and bumping into friends. It seems that everyone from New York comes down to escape the cold winter weather and take in the culture. Glen and I decided that before we parted ways, we would go to the Untitled exhibition to enjoy one last round while hearing ELEW, a rock–jazz pianist-turned-DJ, spin. Just then it hit me: it was 7 PM, I had to fly out in twelve hours, and the closest thing to a cultural experience I had had at Art Basel was walking through the exhibition hall on my way to order a round at the bar. If I hadn't been having so much fun, I would really have had to question my life priorities.

DON'T PEAK TOO EARLY

Each city's social scene and nightlife peaks at a different time, and even those times can change depending on events. Since we each have a limit for how long we can celebrate, it is important to time meals and drinks around that. Work backward from the peak. I generally shoot for dinner to start about four to five hours before, knowing it will last about one and a half to two hours. An example of a New York night out:

8:30 PM–9:30 PM – Start of dinner

10 PM–11 PM – End of dinner, go to next location

1:30 AM – Start to peak

2 AM – Evaluation point

After 2 AM, you should either be on your way home or making it an EPIC night, and at that point, don't forget to enjoy the sunrise.

I am aware that last call is 4 AM in New York, but for the most part, a natural decline in the quality of the experience occurs between 2 and 4 AM.

In the case of New York, if you start dinner and drinks at 7 PM, you would be drinking for almost eight hours by the time you approached the peak. It is doable but very tiring and not necessarily that appealing.

The peak where you live may be a completely different time than the peak where you are traveling. In Buenos Aires, people will often start dinner at 11 PM and go out late into the night. Meanwhile, from the little time I spent in Boston, I noticed that the peak occurs around 1 AM. Whatever the peak time is where you are, make sure to pace your adventure so that you don't peak too early.

With the evening quickly approaching, Glen needed to get ready for an event. In his place, Sophie, a fun-loving and well-connected friend from New York, and her friend Jasmine joined me. Their timing couldn't have been better. Glen was at the point at which he was flagrantly hitting on gallery owners, not noticing or caring whether or not they were married. I will spare him the embarrassment of sharing the details, but it was going over about as well as nails on a chalkboard. I was visibly cringing with every sentence he spoke.

With the exhibit closing, Sophie and I had to make an executive decision as to where our friends would congregate. There were a ton of parties around town, but we had two hours to entertain ourselves before things got started, and we had to eat. We wanted to be at a centralized location, and I knew just the place, so our texts went out: "Dinner at the Gale's Dolce Italian. Shenanigans, tomfoolery, and ballyhoo to follow."

As the group assembled, the lineup was ideal: me, Liam, Sophie, and three of her girlfriends. Among them was Amber, a tall and charming vixen—the little time we had spent together since meeting two months earlier had told me she was adventurous, but I was curious as to just what degree.

Within minutes of sitting down, Liam and I were up to our usual antics. We had shared our stories so many times our delivery was flawless. We regaled the ladies with tales of drunken transvestites on trains, our time working together as knife salesmen at Cutco, and debaucheries and life-threatening travel around the world. As bottle after bottle of wine was poured, we knew the night was destined for insanity.

Amber sat at the far end of the table, and with every glimpse I stole, I had this terribly wonderful thought: I was in trouble. Yes, of course she was pretty, but it wasn't that—she had a rare mix of charm, wit, and naughtiness. The kind of girl you want to bring home to meet Mom, make out with at a dance club, and make breakfast in bed for the next morning. A triple threat . . . of sorts.

To see how far we could take this group, we had to understand how prim and proper they were. Could they handle talking about sex, sneaking into parties, lying about who we were? We needed a litmus test, and that night, it would be initiation into the DPC, and Liam just so happened to be one of the cofounders. "What is the DPC?" you ask. In the spirit of using Snapchat only for "dick pics" (as it was originally intended), the Dick Pic Club involves

LEVERAGE TECHNOLOGY IN THE RIGHT WAY

The question is: When you engage with your phone, is it advancing your experience, or is it because you can't help yourself? How are you using technology? Much of the time, it functions as a distraction. It causes people to focus on something other than the people they are with and the experience they are currently having. This may be unavoidable. At times, you have to communicate with people to let them know where to find you, or you have to search for the place you are going to confirm the address. The question is, When you do engage with your phone, is it advancing your experience, or is it because you can't help yourself?

The mere presence of mobile communication devices shape relationship quality in dyadic settings. In both, we found evidence that they can have negative effects on closeness, connection, and conversation quality. There are few greater gifts than the opportunity to spend quality time with extraordinary people, so don't deny yourself that chance because you were answering a work email on a Saturday at 11 PM that no one was expecting a response to anyway. Technology should contribute value by helping you get somewhere, discovering interesting options, or playing group games like Heads Up!, so make sure that when you do use it, it is adding value.

drawing penises on every photo you take. It is sophomoric, stupid, offensive, and amazingly fun. They loved it, and minutes later crudely drawn penises were flying across our phones.

As our meal came to a close, we had to make a move, but where to go next? It was no accident that we chose to have dinner at The Gale. *Paper* magazine was hosting a rooftop party. Unfortunately, as we took in the scene, it was obvious this event was a dud, and we needed to get out of there. The group was still on high from an amazing dinner, but if we didn't keep the drinks pouring, we would hit a lull, so I made a call: "We are splitting up into two cabs and going to the StyleCaster party at Nikki Beach. I'll take Amber and Jasmine. Liam, go with the other two."

LET'S GET PHYSICAL

When thinking about amusement, we tend to consider options in which we passively enjoy a show, comedy act, play, movie, etc. These can all be fun, but they encompass a small number of possible options.

Consider instead activities in which we are participants, like a game of midnight baseball, a dodgeball bonanza, an air-guitar championship, or karaoke. There is a camaraderie that builds from being physical and participating in activities. They not only provide entertainment and enjoyment, they also bond people.

Amber, Jasmine, and I hopped in a cab, and without a moment to lose, we started sending insane DPC photos from the backseat. Moving to the great music playing on the radio, I took the opportunity to give Jasmine the lap dance of her life. It was starting to hit me that I might have underestimated how much wine we had at dinner, and we were heading for mayhem as we edged closer to the StyleCaster open bar.

On arrival, it was clear that the rain had kept people away, but that was fine since we had brought the party. Liam and I collected shots from the open bar and led the group onto the dance floor. Like a well-trained troupe of bar mitzvah dancers, we showed the all-too-sparse crowd what it was like to "get down to get lucky!" Sophie was rockin' the dance floor, pulling out moves I didn't know existed, while Amber and I spun, dipped, and flirted away. Twenty minutes later, it was time to move on. Even through the cheap pair of Nikki Beach glasses they had given me when I entered I could see the crowd wasn't getting any better. Usually the more I drink, the better the crowd gets, so it was clearly time to leave.

Since there was no Uber at the time, Liam was making arrangements for us to be picked up. In the meantime I was preoccupied with the flirting going on between Amber and me. Was I at a point at which I could make a move?

In these situations, the geek in me comes out and I think of Schrödinger's cat. (See next page.)

At that moment, the potential between Amber and me was both alive and dead, and the only way to know for certain was to make a move and open the box.

While the rest of the group attempted to pack themselves into the cab, I pulled Amber aside and dipped her, and in a ritual as old as our species, I leaned in for a kiss. But for anyone who has attempted a kiss, you know that a kiss isn't just a kiss; it is a question to which we tie our self-worth and value. It is a question filled with doubt, hope, and excitement. The time between the moment you move in and the moment you discover if the other person is reciprocating can feel like eternity. But when I opened this box, what I saw was not what I expected. Judging by the length of the pause, the cat and my ego were both going to need doctors. She jumped up and said, "I'm not going to kiss you when you're wearing those silly glasses!" And like that I had my answer: it was not going to happen.

When we finally managed to squeeze ourselves into the car, I realized it was midnight. It had been almost eleven hours since I met up with Glen, and it didn't look like things were going to slow down anytime soon. More important, I had to leave for the airport in four hours. It was time for us to class it up. The next stop was Chez Andre at the Rec Room, an intimate and upscale lounge back in the lower level of The Gale that reminds you of a basement belonging to a 1970s rock star. Thousands of records line the walls, and the shelves are covered with period knickknacks like lunch boxes, board games, and binoculars.

I knew that if I was going to recover from the debacle with Amber, we needed to do something daring together. We luckily bumped into my friend Allegra who worked there, and in a moment of drunken creativity,

SCHRÖDINGER'S CAT AND UNCERTAINTY

In 1935 Nobel laureate Erwin Schrödinger presented a thought experiment that managed to make the jump from the world of science to pop culture.[39] It all began with the Copenhagen Interpretation of quantum mechanics, which claims that until you observe a particle, it exists in every possible state. Essentially since a particle can be in one of multiple places until it is observed, you must assume it could be in all of them, even if the chances are small.

Schrödinger's thought experiment wanted to poke fun at this idea and show how unrealistic it is.[40] He suggested we consider a locked box that contains a cat, radioactive material, a Geiger counter, a hammer, and a vial of poison.

If the radioactive material decays, it will trigger the Geiger counter to release the hammer which in turn breaks open the vial of poison and kills the cat. According to the Copenhagen Interpretation, the radioactive material is both decayed and not decayed until it's observed, meaning the hammer both broke and didn't break the vial, and the cat is simultaneously alive and dead while the box remains locked. It isn't until we open the box that we determine definitively whether the cat is alive or dead. Otherwise, according to this interpretation, it is simultaneously in both states—alive and dead. Schrödinger thought this was absurd; the cat must be either alive or dead.

Even though Schrödinger was attempting to demonstrate the foolishness of the Copenhagen Interpretation, I think it demonstrates many of the uncertainties in our daily lives. There are things in life that you can never know what state they are in, unless you take action and open the box; until that point we are in a state of uncertainty where we constantly question what would have happened or what could happen.

---

39 Melody Kramer. "The Physics Behind Schrödinger's Cat Paradox." *National Geographic*. August 14, 2013.news.nationalgeographic.com/news/2013/08/130812-physics-schrodinger-erwin-google-doodle-cat-paradox-science.

40 John D. Trimmer. "The Present Situation in Quantum Mechanics: Schrödinger's 'Cat Paradox' Paper." *Proceedings*, American Philosophical Society, Vol. 124, No. 5 (1980): 328. http://www.jstor.org/stable/986572?seq-1#page_scan_tab_contents.

I said, "Alli, I am going to steal the lunch box off the shelf. Expect a meal delivered in it when you get back to New York."

She laughed and made one requirement: "Don't get caught!"

Amber and I had a plan: although a security person stood right by the shelf displaying the box, she would distract him as I moved it to a lower shelf out of sight. Then while I distracted security, Amber would grab it and shove it under her jacket, and we would make our escape. Like the cast of an Ocean's movie, our execution was flawless, and we made our escape to the street with our plunder in hand. Liam and Jasmine followed us out, thinking we were leaving. The obvious question was, "What's next?" And as if he had read my greatest desire, Liam announced, "We are going skinny-dipping."

Still excited from our criminal act, Amber and I ran to the beach, threw our clothes off in a pile, and hit the water. Liam and Jasmine were close behind. The playfulness between us was obvious. Picking her up and tossing

IS THE JUICE WORTH THE SQUEEZE?

Traditional thinking would have you consider whether the effort is worth the outcome. If you get caught doing something that will get you in trouble, is the potential outcome worth the risk? It is reasonable to think about life in such a way, but it isn't how adventurers see the world. To us, it is the risk that makes the squeeze worth it. It is because we might get caught that we dare the attempt; any juice we get is just an afterthought, a prize we get to keep. The real reward is the excitement, the growth, and the challenge itself. If there are serious consequences, it might be a bad idea. You have to decide for yourself, but traditional thinking doesn't always work. The reason to do something isn't just the reward at the end; it is who you get to be when you do it.

her into oncoming waves, I could feel the anticipation building. After about an hour of splash fights and swimming, we made our way back to our things.

The breeze was making her shiver. Wrapping her naked body in my shirt, all the while warming her in my arms, I smiled down at her. The moonlight made her eyes sparkle, and I knew that if Hollywood had ever designed a perfect moment for the hero to lean in for a kiss, it wouldn't hold a candle to this one. And so for an all-too-brief moment, her lips met mine. Finally, after a night of confusion, mixed signals, flirtation, and frustration, I had an answer to that eternal question that has haunted men for millenia: Does she like me?

As the other duo made their way up the sand, she pulled away slightly, and that's when the entire evening between us finally made sense. She was incredibly shy about PDA. I was relieved to figure out what was going on, since all too often we are left searching for an explanation when things don't work out.

We began to dress, and that's when we realized there was a problem. Jasmine couldn't find her purse. Liam's phone and wallet were gone. We panicked, realizing we had been robbed. We were no longer amused. Jasmine was beside herself: her purse had her passport and her grandmother's pearl necklace. I was missing a fortune in electronics. In the midst of all the confusion, Amber said something that was so charming I could have married her on the spot: "Guys, it's just some phones and some money. It was a really great night, and I had a ton of fun. That's what counts."

When Jasmine started crying, I realized I had to take action. "I want you all to get dressed and search the area, specifically trash cans. The thieves may have taken the cash but thrown out the wallets. I'll run to the boardwalk for help."

I was barely able to put my pants on as I arrived at the boardwalk. Noticing two women walking by, I waved them over and explained, "I'm so sorry to bother you, but I just got robbed, can I use your phone to call the police?

One of them passed me her phone, but I couldn't understand what to do. Was I in shock? No, the phone was in Danish, and I had no idea how to use it. With their help, I called 911, and the police were on the way. In the meantime, the rest of the group joined us. They had found everything, except for our phones and cash, strewn by a bungalow not far away. We were all relieved that we would, at the very least, be able to get on our flights.

YOU MAY NEVER KNOW

Our brains have an amazing ability to derive meaning from and find patterns in our conversations and experiences. The problem is that a portion of the time, the meaning we derive is utterly inaccurate, and the patterns we see aren't real. This characteristic is especially pronounced when there is a strong emotional relationship to the situation we are trying to understand.

Someone you like telling you that they aren't interested in dating you anymore, or getting fired out of the blue, will likely cause you to obsess over why. The problem is that any answers you come up with are probably wrong. You could spend months coming up with comprehensive lists of explanations, but the real reason you got fired was the company couldn't afford to keep you, or the real reason you didn't keep dating the person you liked was that he or she was so insecure that rather than risk your leaving in the future, he or she decided call it off now.

In many cases, trying to understand and figure it out is pointless. What is important is moving on and enjoying your life. If you want to spend your life trying to find answers to unanswerable questions, join a monastery and become a monk.

As if the night couldn't get any more eventful, an oddly familiar man was walking past us with a friend on the way to the beach. Art Basel attracts everyone; could it be who I thought it was? As they came closer, I shouted to them, "Russell Simmons, how have you been?"

He looked over trying to place my face, but as we had never met, he was just confused. So I figured I could win him over with some good advice:

JUST IN CASE

If you were traveling and lost everything you had right now, what would you do? How would you get home or how would you continue traveling?

Do you keep scanned copies of your travel documents in your email account? Have you memorized the number of a credit card that you keep at home? Do you know people you could call day or night, and have their phone numbers memorized? Or do you have a paid Skype account so that you can call anyone you need from a stranger's mobile phone? Do you know where your local embassy is? The bare minimum:

- memorized numbers of people to call (day or night)
- downloadable copies of your travel documents
- downloadable copies of your insurance information
- people who know where you are and whom you regularly check in with
- medical alert bracelet for allergies or conditions

You may want to keep everything in a shared cloud folder like Dropbox and make sure friends or family have access in case of an emergency. It is important to always have a plan in place since you never know when you might find yourself stuck with nothing.

"Hey, Russell, I don't recommend going to the beach. We just got robbed."

His friend was immediately enthralled, asking questions about our night. But clearly the last thing Russell wanted to do at 3 AM on the last night of Art Basel was talk to a group of half-dressed, wet, and confused strangers. Although his friend was curious about our adventure, Russell was far more interested in how his was unfolding. Not wanting to upset the king of urban clothing, it became clear that we should end our conversation and leave them to their night. Russell smiled at us, said good-bye, and they made their escape.

With an hour before our flights, the girls went off to pack, and Liam and I had to grab my bags and get to the airport. Sitting at the gate, I reviewed the day in my head. It was extraordinary: every step of the way my friends and I had created fun and exciting ways to amuse ourselves, and even though I got robbed, it still remains one of the days I remember most fondly.

A few months later, Liam and I were telling this story, and I mentioned to him, "It was lucky that one of my cards wasn't stolen. Otherwise, how would I have even gotten to the airport?"

His face lit up as if he had made a sudden discovery and said something brilliant: "We are so stupid! We met a billionaire that night. We should have asked him for some cash to go home. There is no way he would have stranded us; he would have been a hero with a great story."

It was brilliant, and so true, but that's the nature of adventure: Each time you go out, you gain knowledge and experience to make the next time more amusing. I learned an important lesson: the next time I get robbed, I just have to make sure to meet a billionaire a few minutes later and ask him for cab money.

You hear that, Russell? Always carry an extra $50 in case I get in trouble. You know I'm good for it.

TAKEAWAYS:

- ☑ To amuse is to hold someone's attention in an enjoyable manner.

- ☑ The ability to amuse can require the development of a skill in order to attain mastery.

- ☑ The 2 AM principle is not bound to a particular time, and your peak can vary depending on where you are. Learn about the city you're in so that you don't peak too early or too late.

- ☑ Unless you're using your phone to enhance your experience, put it away.

- ☑ Don't just be an observer. Actively participate in your adventures.

- ☑ The benefits of the journey drastically outweigh completing your goal. The journey has the potential of redefining who you are.

- ☑ Understanding why people act a certain way is likely futile. The key is in being OK with not knowing or understanding.

- ☑ Memorize or back up important pieces of information in case of an emergency.

CHAPTER 12

INTRIGUE:

THE END OF THE AMATEUR

YOU ARE SCROLLING THROUGH THE FEED on your favorite social media app, and you see an article that someone just posted. The title grabs your attention. It says something like "A man punched a nun and when you find out why, you'll be happy about it," or "This use for a banana will change you life," or "This man dropped his pants at a mall, and what happened next will shock you." For some reason, you are compelled to click the link and read the article, but why? Do you actually care why a man punched a nun, what bananas are useful for, or what actually happened next?

Probably not, but then why did you click, read, and possibly even share the article yourself? It is all because of intrigue. Said simply, you were curious.

So curious you couldn't help yourself. To be more specific, when there is a gap between the information you have and what you are presented with, your brain obsesses about filling in the missing knowledge. You are uncontrollably compelled to find out why the man punched a nun.

To intrigue is "to arouse the curiosity or interest of by unusual, new, or otherwise fascinating or compelling qualities; appeal strongly to; captivate."[41] Essentially you are catalyzing curiosity.

To intrigue is a very powerful approach to fascinate people or draw them to you. The way you dress, speak, tell stories, or answer questions can all induce a state of curiosity. As this curiosity is developed, people are neurologically more interested in you; you stand out and become a puzzle to be understood or solved.

THE SCIENCE OF CURIOSITY

In 1994, George Loewenstein published the seminal paper "The Psychology of Curiosity,"[42] which proposed a new model for how curiosity works. In it, Loewenstein described what is now known as information-gap theory, which dictates that curiosity occurs when there is a gap between what you know and what you are being presented with. Depending on the size of the gap, you will respond with varying levels of curiosity:

- **A small gap:** If the new information is very consistent with your existing knowledge, you will absorb it quickly, requiring no effort and creating no curiosity (e.g., while you step away from watching the game to grab a snack, your team scores; when you return, you might be excited to see the score, but it wouldn't raise your curiosity).

41 "Intrigue." Reference.com. www.dictionary.reference.com/browse/intrigue.
42 George Loewenstein. "The Psychology of Curiosity." *Exotic References.* (New York: Oxford University, 1994) 121-181. www.cmu.edu/dietrich/sds/docs/loewenstein/PsychofCuriosity.pdf.

- **A large gap:** If the information you are being presented with is completely outside your sphere of knowledge, it will be uninteresting and may in fact evoke feelings of fear (e.g., if you are an actor at a cocktail party speaking to someone in manufacturing about a complex molding process, you would be completely uninterested). No curiosity would likely be created and you would want to leave the conversation as quickly as possible.

- **A medium gap:** When the gap in your knowledge is large enough to raise interest but not so large that it is alienating, you will be curious.

Curiosity functions much like an itch you would like to scratch. It creates a painful discomfort that people need to soothe by filling the gap with the missing information.

Through a series of experiments, researchers from Colin Camerer's lab at Caltech, led by Min Jeong Kang,[43] were able to verify that curiosity follows an inverted-U relationship relative to knowledge.

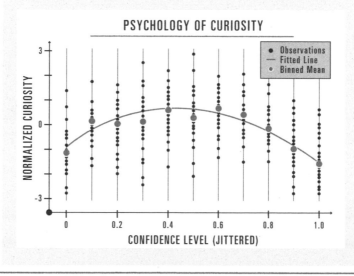

43 Min Jeong Kang, Ming Hsu, Ian Krajbich, George Loewenstein, Samuel McClure, Joesph Tao-yi Wang, Colin Camerer. "The Wick in the Candle of Learning: Epistemic Curiosity Activates Reward Circuitry and Enhances Memory." *Psychological Science*, August 2009, 963–973. papers.ssrn.com/sol3/papers.cfm?abstract_id=1308286.

We are most curious when we know a little about a topic, but if we know nothing or too much, our curiosity declines quickly.

Researchers were able to further demonstrate that when we are in a state of curiosity, our brains activate areas to absorb the knowledge more effectively, creating a disproportionately effective rate of recall. As this process occurs, we absorb not only the information we are curious about more effectively, but also everything else in the environment.

The ability to create curiosity can affect everything from the way you connect with people and how memorable you are to how effectively you teach or present to clients. The key is always in creating information gaps that are large enough to create interest but small enough to be crossed.

You will know that you have achieved a level of competence in intrigue when people tell you, "You are the most interesting person I have met recently."

Creating Intrigue

- It is about information gaps: You are creating a question that others cannot answer without engaging with you.

    a. The gap in their knowledge has to be big and unique enough that it will bother them if they don't understand or get an answer.

    b. The answer has to be simple enough that they can make sense of it. If you need extensive knowledge of quantum mechanics to get the hint, you will lose people's interest.

    c. The gap can be in anything from the way you tell a story to what you do. Almost anything can possess an information gap.

- Speak differently. When people ask you where you live, what do you say? Do you give them the name of your city, or do you take it as an opportunity to create interest and intrigue? I tell people: "I'm from a small island in the Northeast of the United States." Right now you are probably wondering, "What island?" It's called Manhattan, have you heard of it? People often laugh at that and realize we are not going to have a standard conversation. They are intrigued and rewarded for their curiosity. Test it out; come up with new ways to respond to different questions so that you create information gaps, e.g. "What do you do professionally?" or "How do you spend your free time?" or "Where are you from?"

- Dress differently. What do you wear that stands out? I'm not just talking about flair; I'm talking about style. When you meet someone who's well dressed or uniquely styled, aren't you curious? Don't they have a magnetism to them that makes you want to have a conversation? Or at least find out more?

- Listen differently. When you are in a conversation, do you ask unexpected questions that demonstrate a unique perspective?

- Don't overdo it. Being intriguing is great, but if everything you say and do raises questions, then you just come off sounding elusive and potentially sketchy. Over time you will learn how much curiosity to create and how often you should be straightforward.

- There needs to be a reward. If you are intriguing people, what they discover at the end needs to be satisfying and worth the engagement. If the discovery at the end is lame or uninteresting, they will feel gypped.

TUESDAY, DECEMBER 31, 2013, 7:21 PM GMT −5,

New York, New York, USA

40°46'53.9" N

73°58'24.05" W

Let me be clear about this and say it in no uncertain terms: I don't participate in amateur celebrations. I am a seasoned adventurer. You probably have experienced an amateur celebration at some point in your life; I know I have far too many times. They involve overhyped events during which people drink irresponsibly, get sick, get into fights, and often walk around complaining that they aren't having fun.

In New York, the three worst amateur celebrations are:

1. New Year's Eve;

2. The Saint Patrick's Day Parade (correction: any day when the population is proud of drinking);

3. People's birthdays (specifically between the ages of twenty-one and twenty-five).

You will notice it is near impossible to participate in one of these occasions without being disappointed. The problem stems from how much our culture hypes them up and makes people feel they have to "go all out." As a result, reality can never meet the expectations that we have. What would be an otherwise fun occasion ends up disappointing or drama-filled.

PUTTING THE AMATEUR HOLIDAY IN CONTEXT

I know that for many people, celebrating New Year's Eve, Saint Patrick's Day, or their birthday in New York City—or anywhere for that matter—is exciting. There is no doubt it can be, especially the first time. I am not trying to diminish the experience for others at all. Unfortunately, having grown up in New York City, New Year's Eve especially has lost its allure. Think about a popular tourist attraction in your area. You may have seen it fifteen times already. Now imagine that thousands of tourists and locals come to see it on the same day—but here is the catch, they are all drunk, and I'm not talking tipsy, friendly drunk. I'm talking "I-can-barely-stand-I'm-annoyed-at-the-world" drunk. Some of them are even "he-looked-at-my-girlfriend-I'm-going-to-beat-him-up" drunk. Oh yeah, and on top of all of this, you had to pay an exorbitant amount of money to go to celebrate at the same place you always go just to avoid staying home alone.

This is why I have very little patience for amateur holidays, especially New Year's Eve in New York City. Can it be fun? Sure, maybe one or two times. Can it consistently be a pleasant experience? The odds are probably against it. When you hear me make jabs at New Year's Eve in New York City please know I love my city more than you can imagine, but I also dislike New Year's Eve there more than you can imagine.

For years I would avoid the amateur social experiences I suffered during my early twenties by leaving New York over New Year's Eve. Unfortunately, that wasn't always an option. Sometimes fate conspired against me, and I would find myself in NYC avoiding the countless emails and texts asking me, "What r u doing 4 NYE?"

THE ALEXANDER TECHNIQUE—
HOW TO TRESPASS
(LESSONS FROM LIAM ALEXANDER)

Whether you are walking around an off-limits area in a building or a construction site, or sneaking backstage at an event, these ground rules will guide you through it safely:

1. Walk confidently no mater where you go. Most people won't notice you or will feel too socially uncomfortable to question what you are doing there. Remember: Most employees, aside from security, don't get paid enough to care, and the larger the environment, the more they are used to random people being around.

2. If you are stopped, be incredibly friendly. Always make sure you have a slightly vague explanation. Examples include:

   a. "I was told by one of the guys outside that I could come in." If asked who: "Frankly, I don't remember. He never gave me his name, but he was really nice and friendly. Well, I have to finish my _____, I hope your work goes well." Walk off normally and don't make eye contact.

   b. "I'm here to drop something off for Steve [or any arbitrary common name]." If pressed: "I work with his friend, and he asked me to do it as a favor."

3. If called out on trespassing, admit nothing and act very confused and apologetic. "I am so sorry. I thought I was in the right place" (you may want to confirm the address and give one a few blocks away or switch the building numbers), or "I was told I had permission. This is really embarrassing. I am so sorry for any inconvenience. I'll show myself out."

4. You have to play the role of someone who truly believes you're allowed to be there or do whatever it is you were doing. You have to express the embarrassment and show that you feel awful about the confusion and for taking up their time. If you make them think you feel bad enough, they will feel bad for you.

Note: Although there is a real chance of getting arrested, most places will simply kick you out or ask you to leave when you are caught trespassing. If the place is prestigious enough, the staff won't want to get the police involved, because they won't want to draw attention. If it is a house party, even if people realize you aren't supposed to be there, most are non-confrontational so they won't say anything. The most common risk is that of embarrassment and awkwardness. If you are OK with that, then go for it.

This year I had an ace up my sleeve. It was a flash of genius that could redefine the amateur celebration for my friends and me.

On December 31, 2013, I had a plan: make no plan.

Brilliant, isn't it? If the problem with amateur celebrations is the excessive or unrealistic expectations, by making no plans, you can't have expectations. Even if you make the best plans, you are still going to have to live up to them. It is hard enough to accomplish that on a random day, but on a day where no plan can match some insane ideal, it takes an exceptional group to pull it off.

IDENTIFYING AND BEFRIENDING THE RINGLEADER

1. He or she is often the physically largest person or has the largest personality.

2. Look for the loudest one in the group.

3. Seek out the person everyone goes to for instructions.

4. He or she is the one who doesn't follow social norms and thus is more daring.

5. See who has the most physical contact with the rest of the group members.

6. He or she is often dressed a little differently or stands out a bit.

This person functions as a linchpin. If you want to hang out with the group, take them with you, or leverage them to do something else, the ringleader is the one that ultimately makes the call. He or she is the one who has the largest vote for inclusion, so learn to connect with and win him or her over.

And so it came to pass that on December 31, 2013, Liam and I escaped the trap that had plagued our species for more than two millennia. Frankly, we didn't know what would happen, but then again we didn't really need to. Together we were like the MacGyvers of adventure. We could turn a deck of cards, powdered milk, nail polish, and a carafe of wine into the most exciting evening of a stranger's life. But I'll tell you about our double date with the Langshaw twins another time.

The only tentative plan we had was that an old friend, Parker, and a girl-friend of his might stop by at about 10 PM to say hello. As 10 PM came and went without a visit, we began to have our doubts. Parker wasn't messaging us, and we had no idea what we were going to do to make the evening great.

The only things we did prepare were some fun outfits, bow ties included, to bring in the New Year with style. After all, my doctor always said, "Bow-ties are cool."

At quarter to eleven, Parker finally showed up. Apparently dinner had run late. After a short catch-up, he suggested that we visit a low-key celebration his friend was hosting about ten blocks away.

Grabbing a couple of bottles of champagne for our host, we made our way to Ninety-eighth Street. Walking over, my friends were so enthralled in conversation they hardly noticed a large group walking next to us. In fact, my friends didn't even react when I pushed us into the middle of the group, entered a random building with them, and walked past building security unnoticed.

The building was decadent: marble covered the lobby from floor to ceiling, and a full security staff monitored the hallways and entrance. I had no idea where we were but clearly whoever lived here enjoyed their privacy. While in the elevator, Liam picked up on the fact that we were not supposed to be there and started chatting up the people around us. Since we had no idea what we were walking into, I wanted to make sure I had some allies. In groups this large, I try to find the girl who is the most socially gregarious, the one who is always up for meeting new people and loves to bend the rules. Once I spot her, I befriend her as quickly as possible.

Scanning the elevator, I was not surprised to find that she was the one dressed in all the absurd New Year's attire (paper top hat with sparkles, silly glasses, and a dress so reflective that if she weren't skinny, she could have doubled as a disco ball).

Upon entering the apartment, Parker and his friend still didn't realize we were crashing this party. Thinking they were at his friend's apartment, the two went in search of him.

In the meantime, Liam and I explored this charming three-bedroom apartment. Fifty or so people filled the rooms and halls, making it difficult to move around. By the time we reached the back, it was clear to everyone we encountered that we were uninvited guests, mostly due to the fact that we were not musicians in the philharmonic orchestra like all the other guests. With my neon-blue pants and our bow ties, Liam and I couldn't have stood out more.

ETIQUETTE FOR CRASHING

Crashing is distinct from trespassing. Trespassing is about crossing a physical boundary like a fence, property line, or the perimeter of an off-limits area. Crashing is crossing a social line created by a community that is congregating for an event.

Here are some guidelines:

1. **Introduce yourself.** This is not a must, but it can be a good idea if the event is small, and it is clear you shouldn't be there. It will acknowledge the awkwardness and tension that might be developing.

2. **Deliver value.** Don't just mooch off your host. All interactions are an exchange in value, and value can be derived through physical gifts; entertainment; increasing social value; bringing a celebrity element; or making the experience more fun, exciting, or special.

3. **Don't come empty-handed.** It is always nice to show your host a token of respect or appreciation. Just because you are breaking one rule of etiquette doesn't mean you should break all of them.

4. **Politely leave.** If asked to leave, apologize and leave politely. Never get defensive or try to justify anything. This is their event or special occasion, so respect the fact that you are an interloper and leave.

5. **Understand scale.** There is a difference between crashing a thirty-person house party and a 500-person beach party. Intimacy and group size make a

big difference. The smaller the event, the less security will be there, so it is easier to enter, but at bigger
events you can go unnoticed once you are inside.

6. **Get a sense of ambiance and atmosphere.** Not all
environments are appropriate. A large party is probably a better event to crash than a dinner.

An awkward tension was building. We could see the guests staring at us and murmuring to one another. We needed to make a choice: How far were we going to take this? Before I had a chance to discuss this with Liam, he said, "I'm going to find the host and introduce myself."

INTRIGUING BEHAVIOR

When you behave out of the norm, your behavior can be
seen as anything from inspiring and curious to insane.
When your actions are curious and nonthreatening, they
entice people to engage. This is especially true if you
demonstrate a skill or ability that others would like to
learn. For example:

- Sabering

- Mentalism

- Freestyle rap or beat boxing

- Physical stunts

- Hypnotism

The options are limitless, so if you have these skills or
others like them, use them to your advantage.

HOW TO SABER

I have sabered countless bottles of sparkling wine over the years and have taught many people how to do it in the process. It is a fun and novel party trick that is relatively safe and gives the person who does it status and a rush of excitement—especially first timers.

BASIC

1. Take the bottle and unwrap the foil from the neck completely.

2. Take your thumb and run it horizontally across the neck of the bottle. You will notice two vertical lines on opposite sides. These are by-products of the production process. We are going to take advantage of this imperfection in the bottle when sabering it.

3. There is a metal cage that prevents the cork from flying out. There is some debate about whether to leave it on or take it off. You can saber it either way. I personally prefer off. If you choose to remove the cage, point the bottle away from anything that can be damaged or anyone who could get hurt. At times you can accidentally pop the cork as you remove the cage.

4. Point the bottle in a safe direction. Important considerations:

   a. The projectile cork surrounded by glass will be moving fast and can be very sharp, so make sure to point the bottle in a safe direction, and don't just shoot it off toward a building, because you could hit people on the street.

   b. Some pieces of glass will fall to the floor next to you so make sure you aren't doing it anywhere people will walk barefoot.

5. Clear the area around you because you don't want to un-intentionally hit someone with the knife or the cork.

6. Hold the bottle in your weaker hand with the seam pointing up, and shake it a little to build up pressure.

7. Take a sword or large knife, and in a single motion, run the blade on the seam through the lip of the neck. The internal pressure, combined with the strike at such a vulnerable point of the bottle, will cause the top of the neck to shoot off with the cork. A flurry of bubbles and wine will spout out and should be poured as quickly as possible, so as not to be lost. The pressure from the bottle should clear all glass shards from the neck, making it safe to drink. Important considerations:

   a. You are NOT chopping off the top. It probably wouldn't end well if you did. Instead, you are running the blade against the glass almost parallel to the bottle in a single motion.

   b. It may take several attempts. If you can't get it to work on one side of the bottle, try rotating it to the other seam and attempting again.

8. Make sure to clean up all shards of glass and find the cork, if you can.

9. The neck will be very sharp and will pierce trash bags, so once the bottle is empty, I take a sheet of tinfoil, fold it several times, and wrap it around the top of the neck to prevent injury.

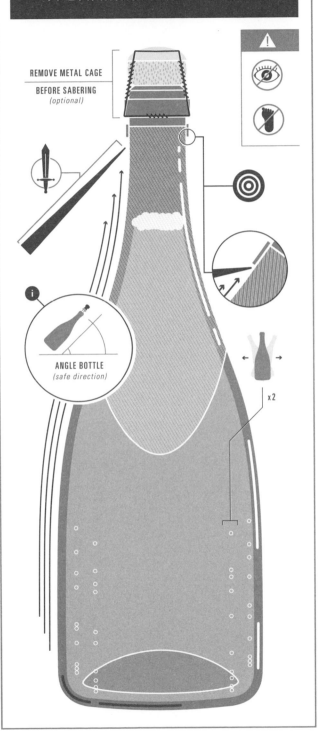

HOW TO SABER A CHAMPAGNE BOTTLE

REMOVE METAL CAGE
BEFORE SABERING
(optional)

ANGLE BOTTLE
(safe direction)

x 2

ADVANCED

It is possible to saber a bottle using a champagne flute or wineglass. That something as fragile as glass can break the thick bottle seems impossible to most people, but about a third of the time I do it this way.

The only difference in the process is that you are holding the base and stem of the glass tight, and you are running the entire base against the bottle with force and confidence.

The upside: It is very impressive, and you can point the fountain of sparkling wine directly into the glass you are holding.

The downside: You have more glass in your hands that can shatter and hurt you, and the flute will often chip or break, so you will have to throw it out.

Note: Please be careful: a small percentage of bottles do shatter. This happened to me at a wedding, and the projectile glass was significant enough to cut my right hand, leaving a scar, and my left cheek, giving me a temporary dimple for a month. I was lucky the injuries weren't worse.

It was a bold move, but the right one, and while he did that, I felt it was only fair to search for our hostess. I found her standing in the kitchen, opening a bottle of champagne for the midnight toast.

I introduced myself with, "Hi, my name is Jon Levy. I have, for better or worse, crashed your New Year's party, but I bear gifts and an experience, and I hope that this would be enough to allow me and my friends to stay and celebrate the countdown with you. I would like to teach you to saber these bottles of champagne we brought."

She was noticeably confused, but who could blame her? A random stranger had entered her home, openly admitted to trespassing, offered her two bottles of champagne, and suggested she take a large knife and chop the tops off of them.

Moments later she was holding a bottle out the window, as I guided her on how to swipe a chef's knife at the neck. The top popped off in a satisfying flurry of bubbles, and she poured us each a flute so we could raise a glass at midnight.

From the other side of the kitchen, Liam gave me a nod. We were golden on all fronts. That's when it hit me: What had happened to Parker and his friend? After not finding their friend, the two just sat on the couch in the living room and kept talking, unnoticed by everyone. They were so inconspicuous and so at home that no one questioned it.

With ten minutes to go before midnight, groups were forming for the countdown. Still standing in the kitchen, Liam and I joined a circle of five girls. Two of these musicians, an attractive blonde named Rebecca and her charming friend, named Sophie, were talking about how they had no one to kiss. Liam pulled me close and whispered in my ear, "Jon, we really can't let these wonderful ladies have no one to kiss at midnight. It would be unchivalrous."

Once these women finished talking, Liam and I offered our services, explaining we would be honored to bring in the New Year by kissing them. The girls looked at each other, smiled, and said yes. As the ball dropped we took our positions, raised our glasses, and at the stroke of midnight Rebecca and I kissed, while Liam and Sophie did the same. It was barely two seconds later when one of the other girls in the circle complained that she didn't get kissed. Liam, of course, being a gentleman, sacrificed himself to the cause.

FLAVOR TRIPPING: A SHOCK TO YOUR TASTE BUDS

Flavor tripping is a by-product of miraculin, a protein found in African miracle fruit. When miraculin binds to your tongue's flavor receptors, it temporarily causes you to perceive flavor differently. It is best known for its ability to make sour foods taste sweet, but from my experience, it also blocks out certain tastes like spiciness and the burn of alcohol.

Since we learn to expect specific flavors from the foods we eat, the experience is incredibly novel the first time you do it.

Some fun things to taste:

- lemons
- sour-cream-and-onion potato chips
- grapefruit
- vinegar
- hot sauce
- stinky cheeses
- pickles
- alcoholic beverages mixed with something acidic (lemon, lime, vinegar, etc.)

GETTING YOUR HANDS ON IT:

African miracle fruit can be easily found online and comes in two forms:

1. **Tablets:** Simply take a tablet of extracted miracle fruit protein and run it on your tongue until it dissolves. After that you are ready to go. The tablet option has a very long shelf life and is highly effective, but it is less aesthetic than the other option.

> 2. **Berries:** The African miracle fruit is a small red berry about the size of an olive and, also like an olive, contains a pit in the middle. You will need to run the juice and pulp of the fruit around your tongue while avoiding the pit. Taking a berry is logistically more difficult, and can be less reactive than taking the tablet, but it is a cooler experience. The other consideration is that the fruit is usually kept frozen, and even then it has a shelf life of only a few months.

So this is where things got amusing: Liam and I kept introducing ourselves to everyone at the party, and woman after woman kept flirting with us, getting intimately close. All of this was beginning to go to our heads. We had never been so popular. Then in a moment of clarity we realized how they saw the situation. Do you remember how I mentioned that we had dressed very dapper? Liam and I were in jackets, bow ties, and crazy-colored pants, with stylized facial hair, and we had walked in together. Versus all the other guys there in button-downs and jeans, we had an intriguing style. They were drawn to speak to us and discover who we were. From their perspective, the most reasonable explanation was that we were a gay couple. We were seen as cool, stylish, and completely unthreatening and uninterested in them. So why not get a bit of attention from some harmless gay couple?

By 12:40 AM Liam and I had spoken to everyone, the party was getting lame, and it was time to move on. Amusingly, Parker and his friend were still on the couch talking, and no one had noticed them. We were ready to call it a night for a slew of reasons, not the least of which was the fact that every guy there was annoyed at us for getting so much attention from the girls.

Out of all the girls we met that night, Rebecca and Sophie were by far the coolest, so after chatting with them for a while, we invited them over to my place a few blocks away for an experience they couldn't resist—flavor tripping, which involves tasting an African berry containing a protein that binds to your tongue and temporarily changes your perception of flavor (e.g., lemons taste sweet, not sour).

Rebecca and Sophie were enticed by the description, so we waved good-bye to my couched friends and, to avoid the cold weather, the four of us hopped in a taxi to my place. Liam poured drinks and I prepared a flavor-tripping feast worthy of this culinary experience (lemons, limes, oranges, kiwi, vodka, stinky cheeses, habaneros, etc.).

INTRIGUING OFFERS

There are some opportunities that sound so appealing and fascinating they draw you in, even if the circumstances that surround them are strange. The curiosity of the experience and the fear of missing out (FOMO) are so great that a person can't help but say yes. The offer in itself serves as an example of your personality and becomes an icebreaker. There are many types of intriguing offers that vary depending on interest and budget. The options are too numerous to list but here are a few simple examples.

- **Food:** African miracle fruit, insects, a Michelin three-star restaurant, etc.
- **Travel:** going on location with Vice, visiting a military base, or simply traveling to another city, etc.
- **Entertainment:** a red-carpet premiere, back stage at a music concert, attending an exclusive after party, etc.
- **Daring:** cliff diving, hunting, bungee jumping, etc.

The experience doesn't have to be outrageous. In fact, many of the things that are banal to you, are intriguing to others—even something as simple as visiting your work, or speaking to some of your friends about their expertise.

When I finally came out of the kitchen, Liam and his new friend were gone, leaving Rebecca and me on our own. In the rush of their relocation, Liam had managed to leave his cell phone.

After the complimentary tour of my apartment, Rebecca and I began to kiss. A few minutes into our make-out session, she said something that surprised me: "This was phenomenal, truly, and you are so hot, but I can't go any further. I hope you understand."

With 2 AM having come and gone, I did what any gentleman would do so late at night: I offered to put Rebecca in a cab, but she wanted to wait for her friend.

So we played the waiting game. While she hung out in my living room watching TV, I excused myself to get ready for bed, ill-prepared for what was coming next. On entering my room, Liam's abandoned phone began to ring. It was Rose, a girl he would hook up with on occasion.

Rose, confusing me for Liam in her drunken state, said that she was coming to "Jon's apartment," where she knew Liam was staying. I attempted to explain that she shouldn't come over, but her phone died before I could change her mind.

Let's recap: Liam is in one room with Sophie, the cute Asian musician; Rebecca, the blonde musician, was in my living room waiting for Sophie; I was in my room getting ready for bed; and Rose was on her way to my apartment expecting to see Liam. Add to this the fact that it was 2:30 AM and I was exhausted. I had to come up with a plan fast before this all blew up in our faces.

When Rose arrived, I quietly pulled her into my room, preventing her and Rebecca from meeting. Unfortunately, her first question was the last one I wanted to answer: "Where's Liam?" she demanded.

"He is on his way. He should be here any minute. In the meantime, I'll grab you some water," I replied, looking for any excuse to leave her in my room.

Exiting my bedroom, I ran to Liam's room to gently inform him that he needed to get up. Sophie was luckily dressed and went to meet Rebecca in the living room.

Standing in his underwear and drinking a glass of champagne, Liam grimaced as I explained the situation and laid out the plan: "Liam, you need

DEALING WITH DRUNKS

Over my years of travels and socializing, I have had to take care of my fair share of drunks. Proper etiquette is not an easy topic to tackle, as there is a wide range of drunken behaviors and circumstances people find themselves in. The complexity is compounded by how well you know the person and how obligated you feel to take care of them. My general rules:

- Don't hang out with people who can't handle their liquor. If someone consistently demonstrates bad drinking habits, don't enable them by spending time with them in a setting that is clearly unhealthy for them.

- Patch them up but don't fix them. You cant reason with someone who is really drunk, so don't waste your time. Just get them to a state in which they can go to sleep safely. You can deal with all the other stuff when they are sober.

- Get them home safe. This is a tough one. If someone is so drunk they could be taken advantage of or start a fight, find someone trustworthy to get them home. I will do this on occasion, but only once per person. If this behavior is consistent, I won't let them come out with me. They need help from someone more qualified than me.

Note: Substance abuse is a very serious issue. Although many of my stories involve grabbing drinks, those who know me know I have very strict rules about drinking, and most important, I never use it as coping mechanism.

to get dressed, including your jacket and shoes. Once Sophie and Rebecca leave, go outside my apartment and knock as if coming in for the first time. Rose will open the door thinking you have just arrived."

We were off to a good start when the girls left, but when Rose opened the door for Liam, there was one flaw: Liam was still holding that glass of champagne. My heart dropped a little. Under what circumstances would someone be walking around the streets of New York, taking a train or even a cab with a full glass of champagne in hand? He might have screwed up a perfect plan, if it weren't for one small fact: it would have taken someone significantly more sober than Rose to notice any of the incongruities.

As they walked to his room, he looked over his shoulder and smiled at me. After fourteen years of friendship, I knew what it meant. We had pulled it off. We had faced off with one of our greatest enemies—the amateur holiday—and we had defeated it.

No more will we or anyone else feel obligated by the burden and expectations from these terrible events. There was now another option. It might not be a perfect solution, but it can work. In specific situations, when expectations run too high, no plan may be better than the best plan. Liam and I later decided that the next New Year's Eve we would take it one step further. We would go somewhere we couldn't have any expectations about, someplace we didn't know. We would go somewhere no one would optionally go. Who knows where we would be standing in a mere 365 days, but wherever it was, I knew that if Liam was there with me, it would be epic.

INTRIGUING STYLE BY
STACY LONDON

How you dress has the power to pull people in and signal that you are interesting and attractive. For those of you who say we shouldn't get caught up in outer appearances, I respect you. Unfortunately, millions of years of evolution and social programming say the opposite. This doesn't mean you should throw out your wardrobe and go into debt for a new outfit; this means that you should ask yourself, "What does my outfit say? What do I want it to say?"

As a favor to all of you, I asked famed fashion expert, author and television host Stacy London to put together the most important fashion tips to insure you have a style that gets the right attention.

1. **The basics:** No stains, no tears, no missing buttons, no unintentional wrinkles, no mismatched socks (it was funny when you were six), no XL free t-shirts you got at a bar or as a tourist. Ya feel me?

2. **Fit matters:** it communicates that you *know* yourself. That you are connected to your body and respect yourself, and people will notice that, whether it consciously registers with them or not. This leads to my next point, which is . . .

3. **Be refined:** Get off-the-rack clothes tailored (it can make them look expensive), or go the made-to-measure (pre-made for your body type) or bespoke route (every detail custom from scratch). If you are over thirty, you must *own* a tux or black suit chic enough to pass for a tux should you be invited to a black tie event. (But really? You should have a tux.)

4. **Quality over quantity:** As you get older, you really should spend the most *you* can afford—but not more—on your wardrobe. Buy fewer items, but make them the best version of that item.

5. **Accessories:** Men don't have tons of accessories, to play with, but that's why it's important to make as much use of the ones available to you as possible: ties, scarves, cufflinks, bags, glasses, even socks. These accents can make the difference between a good outfit and a great look.

6. **Casual:** All of the above may sound too businesslike and stuffy for you. Maybe you're in tech and worth 40 bajillion dollars, but you wear a Dungeons & Dragons t-shirt and the jeans you've had since you were a junior in high school. I'm going to ask you to step it up by doing three things:

   a. I can't state this enough: make sure nothing is too big on you. If you're (unironically) wearing an Atari t-shirt, it needs to fit well. If your jeans are stretched just the way you like them, I'm guessing they either need a belt or ten minutes in a hot dryer.

   b. Get a sport jacket casual enough to layer over the aforementioned tee or even over that brand new, limited-edition *Star Wars* hoodie (I'm not hating on that. I love *Star Wars*. I have a huge collection of the merch myself).

   c. Get yourself one other pair of shoes besides your Nikes or Adidas or New Balance or whatever. Personally, I like oxfords; they're a versatile lace-up so that you can wear them with jeans or with the suit you will definitely need when your company goes public.

7. **Athleisure:** The trick to pulling this off is not to go all in. Mix the hoodie with the sports jacket, the track pant with a turtleneck, or the sneaker with the suit. You get my point. Even a baseball cap can look good with the right suit, but I don't advise attempting that unless you're really advanced.

8. **Hair & skin care:** Yes, you need it! Not just the obvious razor, nose hair trimmer, toothpaste/toothbrush (stick to electric), but it is also important to take care of your skin. There are simply too many awesome and manly men's products in the market now for you not to own the ones that work for you. Same goes for your hair and cologne—find ones the suit you, but never overdo it.

9. **Keep it simple:** Whatever your "uniform" winds up being, the simpler it is, the more versatile it will be for you.

TAKEAWAYS:

- ☑ Information gaps create questions that are big enough to pique your interest, but not so big that you are intimidated by the knowledge. You can create gaps in the way you speak, dress, listen, interact, etc.

- ☑ When the gap is filled, the explanation has to make sense and be satisfying to anyone.

- ☑ Apply the Alexander Technique to— respectfully—trespass or crash events.

- ☑ When an offer is exciting and intriguing, people will have a very difficult time saying no. Consider how to leverage them for group building.

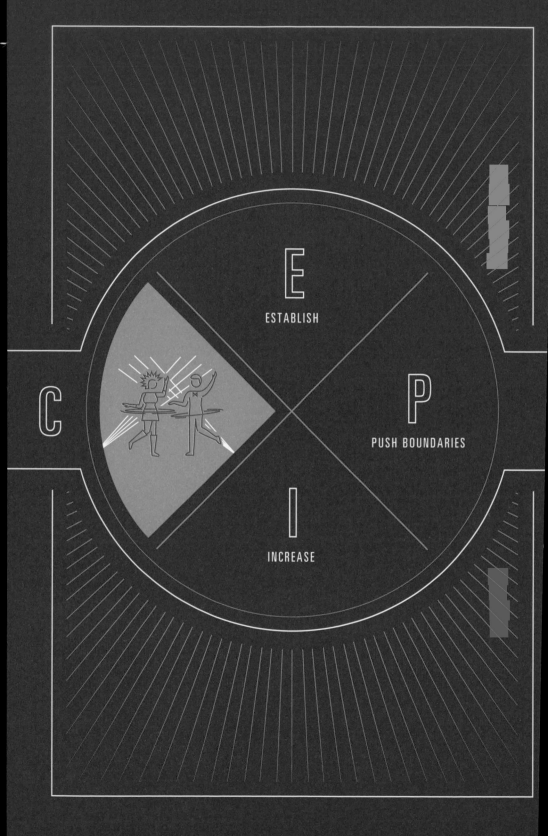

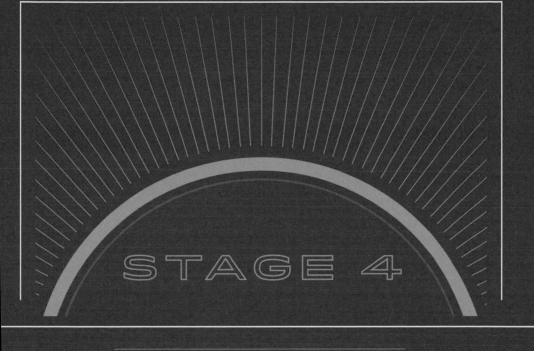

STAGE 4

CONTINUE

"WE MUST BE WILLING TO LET GO OF THE LIFE WE PLANNED
SO AS TO HAVE THE LIFE THAT IS WAITING FOR US."
JOSEPH CAMPBELL

Throughout the course of an adventure you will face many decisions, not the least of which includes deciding where to go, how to get there, or if you should just go home. These are complex considerations. Often it feels like there is no perfect answer. To tackle this issue, we consider the RATE at which we continue.

- · RISK and unpredictability of where we are going
- · ACTIVITY and ambience at the location
- · TRANSPORTATION necessary to get there, or we consider how to
- · END WITH STYLE if it doesn't make sense to stay out any later

The truth is that at the time you are making the decision, it is impossible to know how things will turn out, but taking the RATE into account will put the best odds in your favor.

Once you arrive at a new location, you begin the process again: Since you have already set the basic characteristics defined

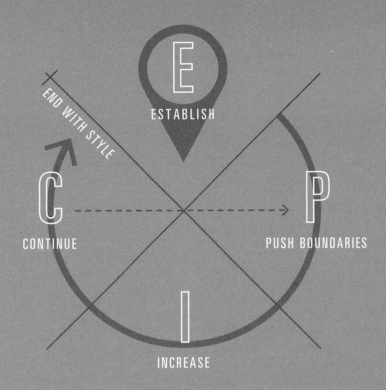

in Stage I (team, mission, constraints, and you have just entered a new location), you move on to Stage II. You enter the location looking for opportunities that will expand your comfort zone. You then elevate and again, until the time you hopefully end with style.

STAGE IV—CONTINUE
SELECT THE NEXT MOVE

RISK AND UNPREDICTABILITY

Manage emotions and group bonding by considering the risks involved in different locations and how unpredictable they are.

ACTIVITY AND AMBIENCE

People rarely consider the breadth of activities they could participate in and the impact of the environment on the group.

TRANSPORTATION

How you get from place to place, the travel time, and the conditions will define the viable options of where to go.

END WITH STYLE

The most important characteristic in remembering your adventures fondly is ending on a good note.

CHAPTER 13

RISK & UNPREDICTABILITY:

THE DILLSBURG EFFECT

WHEN SELECTING THE NEXT LOCATION, you need to consider what you want for your team and how it fulfills the mission. Are you looking to bond as a group? Separate into couples? Does the group need to recover from having done something very intense or are you looking to entice them to cross a new boundary?

When weighing these options you need to take risk and unpredictability into account. Risk is a funny thing: When you take no risk, life is rather mundane; there lacks a catalyst that drives excitement and growth. Conversely, when you take too many risks, you can become overwhelmed. You stress, experience fear, and in extreme situations, you may feel like your life is in jeopardy.

RISKY THINKING

What causes us to take on greater risks? There is no doubt that the people we surround ourselves with, the hormones that flood our bodies, and the environments we are in have a major effect. Remarkably, even the speed at which a person reads can dramatically alter their inclination to take risks.

In 2012, Jesse J. Chandler and Emily Pronin of Princeton University published a paper demonstrating the effect of accelerated thinking on people's appetite for risk.[44] In the first experiment, individual participants read out loud sentences that temporarily appeared on a computer screen at one of two speeds. Each participant was randomly placed in one of two groups: those who were allowed to read the sentences at a standard rate and those who had half as much time to read them, meaning those participants would have to read them twice as fast. Each participant was then tested to evaluate his or her thinking speed.

This is where things got interesting: Participants from each group were given an opportunity to earn money. After the reading exercise, they played a game in which a virtual balloon and pump were presented on a screen. The participants could pump this digital balloon as many times as they liked, and with each pump they would earn five cents, but if they overpumped the balloon, it would burst and they could not keep the money they had earned.

On average the fast thinkers, those who read the sentences at twice the standard rate, pumped 27 percent more than the slow thinkers did. This of course led to them popping more of the balloons and receiving no money, but also receiving higher payouts when the balloons didn't pop. In essence, thinking faster led to a 27 percent increase in taking on risk.

44 Jesse J. Chandler and Emily Pronin. "Fast Thought Speed Induces Risk Taking." *Psychological Science*. April 2012, 37–374. pss.sagepub.com/content/23/4/370.abstract.

In a follow-up experiment, participants were split up into three groups: slow, medium, and fast. This time they were shown videos, but the fast group's video cut from scene to scene every 0.75 seconds; the medium group's, every 1.5 seconds; and the slow group's, every three seconds.

After participants were tested on thinking speed, they completed a questionnaire asking them to evaluate the likelihood over the next six months that they would participate in risky behavior, such as "smoking marijuana, playing drinking games, having unprotected sex, damaging public property, and putting off assignments until the last minute," and to predict if those activities would have negative outcomes. Results were consistent with the balloon-popping experiment: the faster people think, the more likely they are to participate in risky behavior and the less likely they are to think there would be a negative impact from taking the risk.

If Chandler and Pronin's research tells us anything, it's that we can quickly boost our tolerance for risk and our desire for excitement. If we want motivation and the desire for risk, it is as easy as viewing fast-paced content that will encourage us to think faster. If you find yourself in a situation in which people are taking too many risks, try to calm them down so that they will think more slowly. Hopefully they will get some perspective.

Considering the risk and unpredictability of potential locations may seem very thought-intensive, but you will mostly evaluate it intuitively. Consider going to a nightclub: the only real risk is that you might not get in, but other than that the experience is incredibly predictable. You will drink, dance, and possibly flirt with someone cute. But what if your other options were to go with a famous street artist and learn to spray-paint in an abandoned subway station or to crash a wedding at a prestigious hotel?

These scenarios possess much more risk and unpredictability, and as such, they are likely to be more interesting.

The general rule is:

1. If a group lacks energy and needs to be excited, increase risk and unpredictability but stop before you reach a point at which either the risk is too high or the unpredictability goes from being novel and fun to uncomfortable;

2. If a group has a lot of energy and can keep going, continue. If they need to recover from the experience, reduce the level of risk and unpredictability.

Note: Most people have a low tolerance for risk, so make sure you let your group know ahead of time what is involved. Also, remember that there is a big difference between real and perceived risk. You can increase the feeling of riskiness without actually changing very much in your situation.

TUESDAY, DECEMBER 30, 2014, 2:29 PM GMT −5,

U.S. Route 495, New Jersey, USA

The city disappeared in the rearview mirror as Liam and I drove toward central Pennsylvania. With our dislike of New Year's Eve looming over us for weeks, we created a mission that would force us out of the city: prove that we could have fun anywhere. We had found round-trip flights to Cleveland, Ohio, for $79. You would think that the last place you would go to escape New York City on New Year's is a place where that week's lowest temperature hit −10 °F. but it provided what we were looking for: an environment outside of our comfort zones.

AN EXCITING LIFE IS A MENTAL STATE

Throughout my travels I have spoken to countless people, and overwhelmingly the people who live adventurous lives, or at least participate in exciting opportunities, share one thing in common: Mentally, they are open to the opportunity. They create reasons to have new experiences rather than focus on why they can't. For whatever reason, it seems that some people feel like they don't deserve it, or believe that it's unattainable for them.

The idea that people shouldn't or can't have exciting lives is preposterous. You deserve an extraordinary life by the sheer fact that you are a living, breathing human being. This leaves you with two options: embrace the fact that you deserve to live an exciting life, or be willing to accept opportunities even if you feel undeserving. Either way, go out there and have some fun.

Just as I was going to buy our tickets, Liam called me up raving about something called the Dillsburg pickle drop. It turns out that the 2,500-person town[45] of Dillsburg in central Pennsylvania mimics New Year's ball drop in Times Square by dropping a six-foot-tall dill pickle man, complete with arms, legs, and a face. Let's be honest: who could say no to that? If we really wanted to prove we could have fun anywhere, we needed to stack the odds against us; we needed to go somewhere obscure and start with no friends.

We now had a new destination. We were in uncharted territory. We had no idea what to expect, no clue what type of people would be there or what we would do once we got there. We were risking a lot, but no matter what happened, it would be better than New Year's Eve in New York City.

Three hours later, after unintentionally driving past the town twice because it was so small, we arrived at our motel. Having mostly traveled

---

45 "American Fact Finder — Community Facts." United States Census Bureau.

between major cities, I never considered how small a town of 2,569 people was. It included a pizza place, a diner, a bar—although the bar was really the back of the diner—and a single traffic light.

Excited to explore our temporary home, we quickly dropped off our bags and entered the bar. My usual plan is to go to a local social center, meet people, find out what there is to do in the area, and explore. Within a few moments, it was clear how unaccustomed I was to the social scene. Inside the bar, not including the bartender, there were only three guys, and they were about to call it a night at 9 PM. Besides the self-imposed early curfew of a small-town life, I faced a bigger issue: I had no idea how to relate to these guys. They were really nice, but every time Liam and I brought up the idea of doing something exciting, they saw it as impossible. They were resigned to living a quiet life of occasionally getting drunk with the boys and maybe playing some video games.

If Liam and I didn't want to hang out alone that night, we needed to make a move. According to the bartender, there were several nearby towns and a city that all had larger populations and even something that resembled nightlife. The best odds pointed to Harrisburg. We would have to consider the risks of traveling there. For starters, since we had already been drinking, it would be a hefty investment to take a cab round-trip. We would also be investing significant amount of time—thirty minutes each way and enough time to explore. If Harrisburg didn't work out, we wouldn't have time for an alternative plan.

It looked as though our gamble on Harrisburg had paid off: North Second Street was littered with bars and restaurants. Seeing this, I felt far more comfortable and confident that we would make friends to have some fun with. Unfortunately, what we could have never predicted was that each of the ten or fifteen bars would only have three or four people in it, most of whom were on dates.

With midnight quickly approaching, our last hope was to explore a remote part of the city known for having a club. Leaving the last bar on North Second Street, we spotted a girl in her mid-twenties skateboarding past us with a Hula-Hoop. It was like discovering a unicorn.

Cara, which we would later find out was her name, was clearly the most interesting person we had seen in Harrisburg since our arrival. Waving her down, Liam asked if he could play with her Hula-hoop. In the meantime,

LEARN TO SPOT INTERESTING

When you are in a social situation, how do you decide whom to talk to? I focus on speaking to the most interesting personalities, people who are fun-loving, and who strike me as leaders (it's the fastest way to meet a group). But how do you differentiate them from everyone else? It is impossible to create absolute rules, but here are few ideas that will help.

1. Who is laughing and enjoying themselves the most? Is there a group that is giggling and laughing and clearly having more fun than everyone else? Go have some fun with them.

2. Who is the one person people are pretending not to look at? Scan the room and pay attention to who people stare at every few seconds while pretending to talk to their friends. If a lot of people are darting looks at the same person, there is a good chance he or she will be interesting to speak to.

3. Who is the most put-together? I don't mean dressed sexy or proper; I mean the person who has the most style. Who has assembled an outfit that stands out? It might not be your style, but the fact that they are so put-together probably means they are up to something and are interesting.

4. When people are standing in a circle, where are their feet pointing? I have noticed that feet tend to be directed at the person with the most social clout or the leader of the group.

5. Who is dressed very loud? If this person didn't want to talk to others, they would have likely worn something subtler.

I asked her what there was to do in town. After about five minutes of failed hula-hooping and chatting, Cara invited us to join her at the rave she was going to.

Having absolutely nothing better to do, Liam and I were ecstatic. Raves have never been my scene, but it would be better to be at an interesting party meeting people than going back to the motel feeling like we had failed.

As we walked to the party, we all shared stories, but hers were very different than the ones I normally heard on my travels. Every time she spoke, I didn't really know how to react. When she shared that she had recently lost two friends to heroin, I thought, "How sad," but then she explained how lucky she was not to have an addictive personality, so she hadn't gotten hooked when she tried it. I began worrying about where we were going and who else would be there. The next location was feeling riskier and less predictable by the moment.

We walked up to the rave, and it wasn't so much a rave as it was a two-story house that probably should have been condemned. Cara couldn't have been more excited to be there. She turned to Liam and me, smiled from ear to ear, and announced, "I'm so happy I found a babysitter for tonight so I could come."

I looked over to Liam, wondering if I had heard that right. Was our skateboarding, hula-hooping, heroin-shooting, Tuesday-night-partying friend a mother?

Most people in this situation would consider two options: either enter this house and discover what this rave is all about, or, the smarter option, turn around and go back to the motel. Although I felt there was a high chance I would get robbed or beat up, something told me I needed to see this through.

Upon entering the back of the house, a small group of people in their forties and fifties were congregated in the kitchen drinking beer and doing shots. It raised the questions of how Cara would know them and what kind of people would host a rave in their home.

The group welcomed us warmly and invited us to explore the house. Following Cara to the basement where the rave was starting, I was speechless. What I was picturing when I thought of a rave was a massive warehouse filled with flashing lights, loud music, world famous DJs, and groups of people doing designer drugs. This was a little different: we entered a 600-square-foot unfinished basement reminiscent of a *Saw* film. Twelve people were spread throughout the space, while one person in the middle was twirling glow sticks to the DJ's house beats. Behind the concrete staircase we just descended sat a broken washer–dryer and a shower stall that seemed like it had been used to slaughter a pig.

Looking over to Liam for a read on the situation, I found that he was otherwise distracted: a relatively cute girl had come downstairs and he was about to start a conversation with her. From where I was standing, I couldn't hear what she was saying, but when she spoke, I could see her teeth were clearly rotting from meth. The entire scenario was unsettling; I had no idea what was going on. I wasn't sure if I was about to experience a police raid, a drug deal, or even get robbed.

I walked in on Liam's conversation just in time to overhear the girl say, "Oh yeah, I have been to New York. I once drove out there and scored the best drugs."

I signaled Liam to go upstairs. We climbed up two flights of stairs, and were seemingly transported to a completely different party. With a rave taking place in the basement and a group of older couples hanging out in the kitchen on the first floor, the last thing I expected was a frat party on the second floor.

A group of college students sat on the floor of a game room drinking and swapping stories. One of the guys welcomed us and offered Liam and me a drink. Feeling way too sober considering the circumstances, we gladly accepted. He pulled out a plastic bag full of Franzia wine. He pointed the spout to our mouths and said, "Before you can drink, you have to slap the bag for good luck."

MAXING OUT AN EXPERIENCE

Sometimes it's not about having the most fun, but about taking an experience as far as you can. The focus shifts to having an interesting and entertaining adventure rather than a joyous one. It may end terribly, but it can still be a unique experience you can learn from.

So there we were in central Pennsylvania, having followed a girl on a skateboard with a Hula-Hoop to a rave in a house that should be condemned, joining what felt like a frat party, spanking a plastic wine bag in order to earn a drink. Yeah, what else would I be doing on a Tuesday night?

There was only one thing to do in a situation like this: attempt to suck down enough Franzia to make this feel normal. Sitting in the circle with these students, Liam and I were in our element. We knew how to navigate this scene more effectively. We shared story after story—everything from our time in Iceland to how we took a stranger from Stockholm on a trip to Israel. Considering how unsettling the entire environment was, it provided a sense of stability to win some people over. It also didn't hurt that after a few more bag spanks, the Franzia was working its magic.

Eventually, Liam and I went down a nearby hallway in search of a restroom. As we did, one of the guys in the circle yelled, "You will need a guard." I didn't understand what that could possibly mean until we reached the bathroom. I don't know why I would have been surprised by anything in this house, but the bathroom door had been kicked down, requiring anyone who used the facilities to have someone stand guard and shield them from people walking by.

We took the opportunity to walk through all the floors again. The rave had doubled in size, now that Cara had joined the only other person on the dance floor. The older couples on the first floor were still welcoming guests and having drinks. We were feeling safe and at home, and that was a clear sign we should leave. There are certain situations I should not feel comfortable in, and this was one of them.

As Liam and I walked the mile to the cab station, we recapped the night. The house rave had turned into an amazing experience. Each person had a unique story that exposed us to an aspect of American culture we would have otherwise never encountered. The house, although disturbing and strange in more ways than I can recount, was actually quite extraordinary. It was a central location where all those on the fringe of Harrisburg culture could congregate and be included. Regardless of your scene or style, you were welcome. There was something really wonderful about that—a sense of radical inclusion—but I only wish that what had brought these people together was something more inspiring than drugs.

DESENSITIZATION

The more we are exposed to a culture or behavior, the less we will find it extraordinary, odd, or dangerous. We get desensitized to it. Many times, this is a good thing. Doctors shouldn't freak out every time they see an injured patient. They should reach a point at which they are calm and collected so they can think straight.

However, there are certain situations in which you want to be uncomfortable, for which getting desensitized puts you at risk. At times, feeling too safe actually puts you in danger. Wherever you choose to go, be aware if you are getting desensitized to the culture or environment more than you should be. You don't want to get so used to being in situations that are very risky that you no longer notice.

This was clearly not a night I would have planned, but that's the nature of adventure. Anyone can have a great time when things go according to plan, but when your gambles don't pay off, you may find yourself in a risky and unpredictable situation. This one worked out, but it could have just as easily turned out to be dangerous, so make sure you have a clear sense of your tolerance for risk.

TAKEAWAYS:

- ☑ The right amount of risk will ensure a fun and exciting experience without being overwhelming.

- ☑ The risk and unpredictability associated with a location plays a critical role in the group's mood and engagement.

- ☑ The faster you think, the higher your appetite for risk.

- ☑ Increase risk and unpredictability to excite the group, and decrease risk and unpredictability to calm them down.

- ☑ Since everyone's tolerance for risk is different, you have an obligation to inform people of the risks they are taking.

- ☑ Living an exciting life is a mental state—embrace it!

- ☑ Engage with people who stand out; they are often more interesting.

- ☑ Not every EPIC experience is a fun party. Many are unique and odd interactions. Learn to enjoy them.

- ☑ Just because you have become accustomed to an environment doesn't mean the risks are gone. Make sure to take stock to avoid real danger.

CHAPTER 14

ACTIVITY & ATMOSPHERE:

WELCOME TO 'MERICA

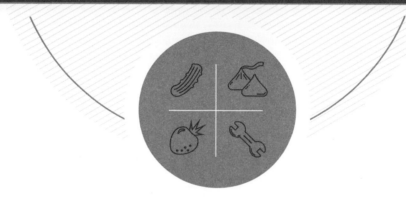

WHILE THE RISK AND UNPREDICTABILITY DEFINE the level of excitement, the activity and atmosphere will define your enjoyment at a new location. Consider what the group wants: Are you simply looking for another bar to have a drink at? Will you take the team for hookah? Maybe you know of a speakeasy that is secluded and more low-key, or a foam party on the beach, or a transgender fashion show. The options are limitless, but not every option is appropriate.

Some people might feel uncomfortable at a transgender fashion show, and that could be a good thing. Others might not want their nice clothing ruined at a foam party. It is easy to ignore the breadth of options and default to the standard activities like barhopping, clubbing, or bowling, but if you want to have a more interesting experience, then open your mind to the possibilities. My brother recently took me and some friends to a street-art spray-painting class—it was incredible, reminding me how fun creative activities are. At my next party, I plan on covering my walls with paper and letting people have a crayon-drawing experience.

When considering activities and atmosphere:

1. Consider what the group needs:

    a. **Keep going:** If it ain't broke, why fix it? The group's energy is good, simply continue with similar activities.

    b. **Energize:** The group is tired, and you need to wake people up and inspire a second wind. Find a way to get people moving phys-ically, or do something as simple as stopping by a coffee shop.

    c. **Chill out:** The group has peaked for a bit and needs to relax.

    d. **Bond:** You want to build camaraderie among people in the group or between you and a specific person. Find a scenario that is you against the world (e.g. sneaking into an off-limits area or invent-ing a social game.) If you need something more low-key try board or card games like Cards Against Humanity. If that's not exciting enough, up the stakes for winning and losing by playing strip poker.

2. If the standard options were no longer an available, what would you do? Throw out the normal playbook and get cre-ative. Would you play a game, see something live (musicians, street performances, theatrical events, etc.), explore a part of your town or city that you have never been to?

This is a great thought experiment. You can always include whatever you come up with in the standard activities so that if you choose to play a game, you can do it at a bar or even on the sidewalk. Now you have expanded the experience and given it depth and novelty.

All of this raises the question of how this fits in with the mission. As long as the activity doesn't oppose the mission, you will be fine. If your mission is to perform three random acts of kindness for strangers, you can spend some of your time exploring unfamiliar areas in your city, but it wouldn't work if the activity involved sitting at home and playing Scrabble with your sister.

A WALK TO REMEMBER

I'm sure you would agree that going to a loud nightclub and going to a spa have a very different effect on you. Both can be fun, but some experiences can drain you, while others seem to restore our thinking and vitality. This raises the question, How much does atmosphere and ambience affect us?

In 2008, a group of University of Michigan researchers led by Marc G. Berman gave us insight into how our environments affect us. These researchers were testing attention restoration theory (ART), which suggests that people can focus more effectively after spending time in nature. ART is based on the idea that our attention has two systems: the involuntary system, which is activated by environmental stimuli, such as a car backfire or a sudden change in temperature, and the voluntary system (aka directed attention), which intentionally focuses on a task, such as reading a book, playing a game, or doing a math problem. According to ART, spending time in nature restores the voluntary system.[46]

In the first of two experiments, Berman and his team took a group of students and administered a series of focus-

46 Marc G. Berman, John Jonides, and Stephen Kaplan. "The Cognitive Benefits of Interacting with Nature." *Psychological Science.* December 2008, 1207–1212. www-personal.umich.edu/~jjonides/pdf/2008_2.pdf.

driven number exercises to assess their directed attention. The students were then randomly assigned to take a mapped-out, 50–55-minute walk in either the Ann Arbor Arboretum, a tree-lined, secluded natural environment, or the heavily trafficked, loud and bustling urban environment of downtown Ann Arbor. Upon returning, students were tested again. A week later, the students returned to the lab, repeated the exercise, and took a walk through the environment they hadn't visited in the previous week.

Researchers discovered that the students' directed attention was significantly improved by the walk in the arboretum but not by the walk through downtown Ann Arbor. In other words, walking in nature made them more focused and effective, while walking through a congested city seemed to have little to no effect.

In a follow-up experiment, the researchers replaced the walk with simply showing pictures of nature or urban settings. Although the results were a bit weaker than those from the actual nature walks, just seeing photos of nature caused enough of a therapeutic effect to increase scores on the directed-attention tests; the photos of urban settings resulted in no significant improvement.

The results of these experiments are fascinating: there is hardly a person among us who would say they are not affected by the activity or ambience they are in, but it is unlikely that we would have ever said that staring at a photo would make us better test takers or more capable of focusing.

This research suggests that when considering environments, activities, and atmospheres, we should take into account how much focus we have. The loud distracting environments many of us have gotten used to may be wearing on us, though the suggested calming effects of a photo of nature may be enough to restore us to some degree.

When selecting where to go next, consider how stimulated people should be. If their directed attention is worn-out, take them somewhere calming and possibly natural.

In the meantime, here is a tree so you can focus more effectively on the next chapter.

40°06'35.7" N
77°02'26.0" W

WEDNESDAY, DECEMBER 31, 2014, 11:24 AM GMT −5,

Dillsburg, Pennsylvania, USA

After previous night's epic rave, Liam and I realized we needed to make a better plan if we wanted to entertain ourselves. After a little searching we discovered that our motel was less than thirty miles from Hershey Pennsylvania, a town famous for smelling like chocolate thanks to the legendary Hershey Chocolate Factory and Hershey Park. The kid in us wanted nothing more than to spend the day at Hershey Park enjoying the rides, and the adult's in us wanted nothing more than to spend the day at Hershey Park enjoying the rides.

By 2 PM we were being serenaded by animatronic cows and learning the history of this great chocolate producer. The most important discovery we made was that, similar to Dillsburg, at midnight the town of Hershey drops a ten-foot-tall Hershey's Kiss. Standing next to this giant ode to cocoa, Liam raised an important question: What if these weren't the only towns that had this tradition of dropping something at midnight?

After a quick search online, we discovered that towns all across America had similar traditions, and within a few miles of where we stood:

1. Dillsburg drops the dill pickle man;

2. Harrisburg drops a giant strawberry cutout in honor of Strawberry Square, where the celebration is held;

3. Carlisle drops a giant town badge, but in previous years, they dropped a miniature Indy race car until, rumor has it, one year it caught on fire;

4. Mechanicsburg drops a giant mechanic's wrench;

5. Hershey drops a giant Hershey's Kiss.

We had a new mission: photograph all five and celebrate the New Year in style. With five hours until midnight, we had plenty of time to pull it off and grab some dinner.

Excited to see all of these outrageous objects, we snapped a shot of the Hershey's Kiss and ran back to the car. Traffic going into Harrisburg was building up as streets were being closed for the festivities. Having parked the car a quarter mile away and received bad directions from several confused locals, we were now twenty minutes behind schedule. But there on top of a building hung the object of our desire: a giant strawberry cutout. We had two out of five, and trying to make up the time, Liam put a heavy foot on the gas—until sirens and flashing lights pulled us over.

At just about 8PM a state trooper walked up to the window and demanded Liam's license and registration. Having rented the car, we passed the trooper all of our paperwork. Upon returning from doing a background check, the trooper demanded the registration again; it turned out that the rental company hadn't printed us a proper contract or provided registration. To make matters worse, even though we had rented the car in New York, it was registered in Pennsylvania, but the registration and inspection sticker had expired.

From the trooper's perspective, he had just come across two guys speeding down a highway in a car that was illegal to drive because it had no registration, and was given some strange story about why the guys in the car opted to come from New York to celebrate New Year's Eve in Dillsburg. The entire scenario was beyond comprehension.

Taking our keys, he went to his car to call for backup. Without a running engine, the temperature in our car quickly fell to 25 °F. Liam and I began to worry because, from what we understood, the trooper had every right to take

KNOW YOUR RIGHTS AND HOW TO REACT

Do you know your rights? If you are pulled over, stopped, and searched, or arrested, do you know what you are supposed to do? Do you know when you should ask for a lawyer and what the police are obligated to tell you?

You may think that because you are innocent, you have nothing to worry about, but more and more we see that justice is not served fairly, and culturally, we are well aware that innocent people are sent to prison all the time, and civil liberties are being eroded. This is not a political statement; it's an important issue I want to bring to your attention. Take some time and speak to a lawyer. Their advice should be free. Additionally, there are organizations that provide education and information.

DON'T LEAVE A DIGITAL RECORD

I know you want to remember all of the craziness that you saw and participated in, but it is *never* a good idea to keep a record of questionable activity. You don't know what might happen to digital photos, and you probably don't want to deal with the ramifications.

If for some absurd reason, you really feel the need to preserve memories, take nonsensical photos that have nothing to do with the situations (e.g., a group photo of people's shoes in a pile is a great reminder of skinny-dipping, or a photo of you and the park in the background can serve as a reminder of sneaking into a closed playground after hours, etc.).

us into the station and impound the car. We would be stuck on New Year's Eve miles from our hotel with no way to get back home the next day. While Liam got the runaround from the rental company, I called my friend and lawyer Jesse Rosenblatt, to let him know where we were in case we got detained. We were in trouble, our cell phone service was spotty, we were cold, and we might be taken in by the state trooper.

When backup arrived, the questioning began again. Not believing our story, they demanded that Liam step out. As they searched him and the car, I had a temporary panic attack. My camera was sitting in clear view, full of photos from the previous night's rave. If they found it, they would come to the reasonable conclusion that Liam and I were drug dealers, because even I wouldn't believe that two guys from New York would randomly accept an invitation to a rave from a skateboarding Hula Hooper. The moment the search was done I deleted some of the crazier photos.

After an hour and a half at the side of the road, a third police car arrived. Apparently, in the Dillsburg area on New Year's Eve at 9:30 PM, the closest thing to a police emergency is two guys in an empty rental car with an

DON'T GET ATTACHED TO YOUR PLAN

The great military strategist Helmuth von Moltke suggested that no battle plan ever survives first contact with the enemy. An adventure is very similar: you can come up with the perfect mission and an ingenious plan, only to discover that none of it makes any sense once you are out of your home, and therefore you need to readjust. Your mission and your plan aren't there to burden you; they are there to give you direction. But even the best of plans fall apart as you encounter unexpected opportunities and challenges. Allow yourself the freedom to explore other options that present themselves. You don't want to miss hanging out with the coolest people you ever met just because you had tickets to see a movie that has been out in theaters for two months. Instead, make new friends and catch it in a few months on Netflix.

expired registration. Even though the temperature continued to drop and a third round of questioning was about to start, Liam and I were in complete agreement: it was still better than being in New York on New Year's Eve.

Fortunately, this new, more senior trooper was convinced by our emails and phone calls to the rental company that we weren't some criminal masterminds about to break bad in Dillsburg. At 10 PM, after two hours of freezing, questioning, anxiety, and confusion, the cops agreed to release us if we drove to the closest rental location to exchange the car.

With only two hours until midnight, we wasted no time getting to Carlisle. The streets were already full of locals celebrating First Night, the town's annual New Year's festival. At the end of the main street hung a large glowing badge several feet across painted with colorful imagery. If this was any indication of how locals participated in New Year's Eve, we were excited. After two hours of sitting in a frozen car being questioned, it was the mood changer we desperately needed.

Mechanicsburg was a bit of a culture shift after the liveliness of Carlisle: no one was out yet and we had to search through the streets to find the wrench, which was in a side alley not yet attached to the crane. The wrench was a massive to-scale replica, about eight feet wide and three feet tall and outlined with glowing lights.

With four down and one to go, we headed home to Dillsburg. Even with our run-in with the law we had eighty minutes to go before midnight. A towering construction crane stood in the middle of Dillsburg's main street holding the pickle man several stories in the air. Looking around, we saw about ten people were present. This was a stark contrast to Carlisle and the setup that was taking place in Harrisburg.

Our mission was to photograph all five items and celebrate in style. We had completed the first part, but celebrating in style was never defined as hanging out with grandma and a seven-year-old. We weren't going to stay in Dillsburg just because that was the original plan.

Liam and I realized that if we threw our things in the car, we'd have just enough time to drive to either Harrisburg or Carlisle. This plan faced an additional problem: we had no place to stay, and this would be a one-way trip since we would be drinking. We were also completely unsure if hotels were sold-out because of the holiday.

CULTURAL EVENTS

Experience tells me that when you are in the midst of a cultural event, people feel a connection to one another that normally isn't there. Think about attending the running of the bulls, South by Southwest, Burning Man, or Coachella. These are centralized experiences that people attended for a specific reason. In situations like these, people tend to be very open to making friends and having conversations with strangers, so don't hesitate to say hello.

Physically and emotionally drained, neither of us wanted to make the call on where to go, so we took the decision out of our hands by pulling a random playing card from a deck—red for Carlisle and black for Harrisburg. Five minutes later we were on the road to Carlisle. Having no place to stay, we parked with less than forty minutes to make friends and find a party to go to. To ensure that we had something to toast with during the New Year's countdown, I grabbed my favorite travel flask from the trunk and we headed toward the center of town.

CARRY A FLASK

For years I have been making my own alcohol infusions. Some are so delicious people come to my parties just to drink them. One of my traditions when I travel is to carry a flask full of a high-quality alcohol. I do this for two reasons and neither of them pertain's to saving money.

1. When you share something as intimate as a flask it is a bonding experience, especially when it is full of something like a homemade infusion.

2. It can be nice to have something to drink and share after last call.

The streets were alive with excitement. Thousands of people congregated around the intersection where the badge would be dropped. The local radio station was blasting music, and a group of college students danced around, drinking and leading a conga line. Liam and I jumped in line to show off our best moves and started making friends as quickly as possible. I struck up a conversation with a recent college graduate, her boyfriend, and a few of their friends and shared the flasks we had brought.

On discovering that we were from New York, they generously invited us to their after-party, which was about a five-minute walk from where

FOMO AND THE BEST PLACE IN THE WORLD

Fear of missing out (FOMO) is the belief that whatever you are doing isn't as good as an alternative option. It is a regret that if you had somehow made slightly different choices, you could be in a better place. Whether it is actually any better is highly questionable, but the belief that it might be is all that is necessary. You could be at the best party in the world, see a friend's photo posted online, and suddenly feel envious and annoyed that you aren't at the event your friend is attending.

Let's be honest here: with more than seven billion people in the world, there is undoubtedly something going on that you would enjoy being at—whether it is any better is a matter of opinion. I live by a very important rule: wherever I am is the best place for me to be in the world. Why? Because I said so, and I am willing to back it up with effort. Also, I can never be where I'm not. It is a fundamental fact of existence.

That being said, there are certain things you can do to prevent FOMO.

1. Stop looking at social media when you are out. It is rude and will only make you envious.

2. If you do look at social media, realize that the people who look like they are having fun probably aren't. If they were, they wouldn't spend ten minutes taking thirty photos and coming up with clever captions; they would be having fun and enjoying the experience they are having.

3. Remember that wherever you are is where the adventure is. It's not always about fun. A lot of it is,

but there are a lot of other elements that go into an adventure, and you need to accept that.

4. Focus on enjoying the experience you are having now. Be present for the extraordinary people you are with.

5. Pick one thing you are experiencing that you are really appreciative of and realize how fortunate you are to enjoy it.

6. Look up stories about people who are less fortunate. The fact that you are reading this book probably means you are in a much better situation than a large portion of the world. Be appreciative that you get to experience the life you have.

we were. A house party was exactly what we were hoping for after all the time we had spent in the cold.

The one-minute countdown began, and Liam and I laughed at how different our situation had been just one year earlier. The previous year we had crashed a party thrown by some of the world's best musicians. This time, when the clock struck midnight, according to the most patriotic country song I have ever heard playing over a PA system, I was "in 'Merica." Fireworks filled the sky, everyone screamed and cheered, and by 12:10AM, the streets were empty and cleanup crews were in full force. The stark contrast to ten minutes earlier was jarring. Momentarily I wondered how my friends back in New York were celebrating. They probably weren't watching street sweepers clean broken glass. They were probably having the time of their lives, but then it hit me: they couldn't possibly; they were in New York on New Year's Eve.

Not wanting to show up to the after-party empty-handed, Liam and I grabbed a bottle of gin by Bootlegger 21 from the trunk and some mixers to give our hostess, and walked to her home. No one answered the front door, so we went around back, thinking they couldn't hear us. After we entered the back door, we knew we were in the right place when we saw one of her friends, William, was passed out facedown on the couch hugging a jug of whiskey.

Hearing some music from above, we made our way to the top floor. The couple and one other friend were sitting around having drinks. Our hostess welcomed us with open arms and promised more people were coming. It was 12:30AM and my sense was that no one was coming, but unfamiliar with the social scene of Carlisle, we respectfully sat on a couch and watched to see what unfolded.

William, woke up from his nap and joined us. He sat near us at the edge of the coffee table. Even though he was so drunk he could barely hold himself up, he still took swigs from his half-empty jug of whiskey. William was a twenty-three-year-old, 5-foot-9, overweight white guy dressed in a dirty band T-shirt and worn-out jeans. In his current state, he was hardly capable of holding a conversation, but that didn't prevent him from trying.

"Wow, you guys are really good-looking," William muttered at us.

Liam thanked him for the compliment.

Apparently quite curious about our friendship, William felt the need to ask if Liam and I had ever made out. Both of us responded in unison that we had not. Trying to be supportive of our friendship, William suggested that maybe all we needed was someone to encourage us. Hoping to put this conversation to rest, I explained that we had been best friends for fourteen years; if it was going to happen, it would have happened already.

And then he said something completely unexpected: "Well, sometimes I think that's what I need, you know, someone to say, 'You're a dude and you're a dude—you two should make out.' Because I don't know if I would have the guts to do it otherwise."

Apparently, William saw hanging out with Liam and me as the ideal time to come out of the closet. Frankly, I can't imagine how difficult it must have been for him that he needed to get so drunk to talk to complete strangers about it. I just hoped that he would remember the conversation the next day.

With the awkwardness building, two things became amazingly clear: first, no one else was coming; second, it was time for Liam and me to excuse ourselves.

Having missed last call at the only two bars in town, everyone was heading home. This was a luxury we didn't have as we had abandoned our

THE SECRET TO
SURVIVING AWKWARDNESS

I know this is hardly a solution, but when I come face-to-face with incredibly awkward situations, I remind myself how fun the story will be in a few weeks, days, or even hours. I collect awkward moments like children collect trading cards because they make the most amusing and universally understood tales.

hotel. There was one last refuge for the nightlife aficionado: the twenty-four-hour diner.

As we entered the diner, we took in the scene. It was utter bedlam. There was only one waitress on duty to serve more than forty people. In between taking orders, dropping them off, and taking care of checks, she had to break up a fight and deal with drunk, upset customers. It seemed the one thing she couldn't do was answer the phone that was ringing continually.

To help out this stressed waitress, I answered the call: "Carlisle Diner, how can I help you?" The young lady on the phone thought she had left her wallet in a booth. I emailed her a snapshot to confirm where I was looking, but I couldn't find anything.

After finishing our meal and closing out the bill, we found a hotel and went to bed. The next morning I received an email from the girl who had lost her wallet at the diner. She said she'd heard we had gone to her friends' New Year's after-party and hoped we had had fun. It was an amazing coincidence, but I guess that's how it is in 'Merica. People's lives intertwine in really random and interesting ways. When you leave the confines and familiarity of home, you discover cultures and participate in activities you may have never imagined. I loved my visit. The people I met were kind and generous, and they exposed me to a new perspective. That is almost always a good thing. But most important, anything is better than New Year's Eve in New York.

DINERS

I couldn't have a book about adventurous experiences without paying homage to late-night diners. They are there for us at the end of the night, when we are exhausted and hungry and wanting nothing more than to laugh with friends as we overindulge. They are also there for us the next morning, when what we need is orange juice, coffee, and the greasiest meal you could imagine.

I want to thank every diner employee who I have had the pleasure of encountering. You have made my days and nights amazing. Thank you.

TAKEAWAYS:

- ☑ When selecting a new activity, be aware of people's comfort zones. Stay attuned to what your team needs and use that to define the next activity or atmosphere you should be in.

- ☑ It is easy to rely on familiar activities like barhopping, bowling, going to a restaurant, etc. Don't ignore the breadth of options available to you simply because it takes some effort to discover them.

- ☑ Connecting with nature or even staring at pictures of nature can restore your focus.

- ☑ Don't document or photograph the stupid or illegal things you do. Instead, take photos of completely innocuous things that can remind you of what happened.

☑ In case you get in trouble, make sure you
know your rights and how to react to law
enforcement officials.

☑ Carrying a flask is a great way to bond with
strangers and to ensure you can have a drink
after last call.

☑ Cultural events provide a highly effective
common ground to connect with people.
Attendees are more open, celebratory, and
ready to engage with strangers.

☑ Remember that wherever you are is where
the excitement happens.

CHAPTER 15

TRANSPORTATION:

SHOPPING FOR ADVENTURE

T'S 10:00 PM ON A SATURDAY night. You are out with a group of friends having a great time, but the place where you are hanging out is winding down. Everyone wants to go somewhere else—but where?

- There is no designated driver, so your cars are out of the question.

- The women in the group are wearing high heels, so you can walk a maximum of two or three blocks before the mood shifts from festive to painful.

- It may start raining at any moment, or it is so hot that being outside for more than a few minutes is miserable.

- You know about some parties, but they are twenty minutes away by cab or public transportation. Can you keep people interested for that long?

Transportation is easily one of the most logistically complex aspects of an adventure. Anyone can go to a bar, but to coordinate moving a group of people across a city can be a nightmare. Here are some basic guiding principles to prevent issues:

- Walking:

    a. Sneakers: A half mile or more, depending on the payoff waiting for you at the end of your journey.

    b. Heels: At most, two to four city blocks, which is about a tenth to a fifth of a mile.

- Cab/Car: Ten to fifteen minutes maximum (unless you are headed to your final destination). It is hard to keep the mood upbeat for more than fifteen minutes when you are in a car.

- Weather: Don't let people get wet, freeze, or boil.

Those are just the basics, but with some creativity and experience you can master transportation. Mastery is achieved when you have the transportation method become part of the adventure.

- Want to get around Budapest? Use a bicycle bar, where ten people sit at a moving bar that is powered by their pedaling. See the city while having a beer.

- Need to get food and drinks from the supermarket to your home? Race shopping carts.

- Need to get between neighborhoods in New Orleans? Hire a jazz band and a police escort. A mile-and-a-half walk feels like a dance party.

- Need to get to your hotel in Tokyo from the airport? Take a helicopter so you can enjoy the skyline. Time it right and see the sunset in style.

- Have to visit a nearby city? Take an airplane pilot class and fly to your destination.

- Rather than taking public transportation to get around Croatia, hire a boat and a skipper and sail between the islands on your own timeline.

If those options sound expensive:

- take over a train or subway car with your friends and turn it into a dance party;

- turn a car ride into a race;

- turn a cab ride into a game of Heads Up!;

- turn a walk into a cappella or karaoke sing-along;

- devise a bar crawl or scavenger hunt so that people have a reason to go from one place to another.

The options are limitless; the key is to change your perspective. Transportation is not a chore; it is a celebration, a continuation of the experience, an opportunity to meet interesting people, or, if you need a few minutes to recuperate before the next activity, time to take a nap.

YOU AREN'T
THAT INTERESTED

How long does it take for people to lose interest? Researchers have estimated people's attention spans to be as short as a few seconds and as long as twenty minutes.[47] Dr. William McKeachie, former president of the American Psychological Association, estimates it at about ten minutes based on students losing focus during lectures.[48] At this point they have to reengage to last another ten minutes. With an average of ten minutes until boredom, it is no surprise that when we go from one place to another, it is hard to maintain high energy and interest; there is very little to engage with.

It turns out that the issue is more complex than being bored or not. Research led by Thomas Goetz at the University of Konstanz in Germany has found that there are five different types of boredom. They range from indifferent boredom, which can be almost pleasant since it reflects "a general indifference to, and withdrawal from, the external world" to reactant boredom, in which people "leave the boredom-inducing situation and avoid those responsible for this situation (e.g., teachers)."[49]

In fact, boredom can be experienced as so undesirable that when researchers gave people the choice between waiting in a quiet room (no cell phone, nothing to read, no music, etc.) for up to fifteen minutes or self-administering a mild electric shock, many—predominantly men—chose inducing pain over being alone with their thoughts.[50]

47 Dianne Dukette and David Cornish. *The Essential 20: Twenty Components of an Excellent Health Care Team.* (RoseDog Books, 2009), 72–73.

48 William McKeachie. *Teaching Tips: Strategies, Research, and Theory for College and University Teachers, 10th Edition,* (Houghton Mifflin, 1999) 7–79.

49 Thomas Goetz, Anne C. Frenzel, Nathan C. Hall, Ulrike E. Nett, Reinhard Pekrun, and Anastasiya A. Lipnevich. "Types of boredom: An experience sampling approach." *Motivation and Emotion,* 38, no. 3 (2014): 401–419.

50 Timothy D. Wilson, David A. Reinhard, Erin C. Westgate, Daniel T. Gilbert, Nicole Ellerbeck, Cheryl Hahn, Casey L. Brown, and Adi Shaked. "Just think: the challenges of the disengaged mind." *Science,* 345, no. 6192 (2014): 75–77.

Predictably, transportation is not the most entertaining activity. Going from one place to another lends itself to the least amount of control and the greatest risk of boredom. How should you deal with this? First off, carry a Taser with you so when people get bored they can electrocute themselves. More important, know the upper limits of transportation time. Avoid moving a group if it will take more than ten to fifteen minutes, because you will enter a range that could leave people bored or wanting to go home instead of continuing on. Of course at times this is not an option; sometimes your destination is farther away. In these cases, you shouldn't worry too much about it, because it is not your job to make everyone happy all the time. But in general, timing should play a big role in informing your decision of where to go next.

SATURDAY, AUGUST 1, 2009, 9:34 PM GMT −5,

New York, New York, USA

40°46′53.9″ N

73° 58′ 24.05″ W

I never understood how to leverage transportation until my old college friends Roxie and JT wanted to go out for dinner in Manhattan's West Village. The three of us met at my place on the Upper West Side and took the subway downtown. Most of the time when I get on the subway, I see it as a chore. But for whatever reason, the three of us were in an especially playful mood, and when we got on the train, we started singing for everyone around us. I don't know if we looked down on our luck, but one woman confused our enchanting melodies for panhandling and gave us money. We spent the remainder of the ride trying to convince her that the money should go to a more worthy cause.

Getting off at the Fourteenth Street and Seventh Avenue subway station, the three of us made our way to the Dallas BBQ on Eighth Street. If you

THE RELATIONSHIP BETWEEN FUN AND MONEY

In my travels, I have had the opportunity to stay in opulent palaces and sleep on park benches. I have eaten foods that cost more per bite than some people pay in rent, and I have eaten street meat in foreign countries that would scare you. Throughout all these experiences, I have almost never noticed a significant correlation between how luxurious or expensive something is and how much fun it is.

Don't get me wrong: Luxury is wonderful. It makes you feel special. Professional chefs produce delicious food. You will likely enjoy a wine more that you are told is expensive regardless of its actual cost.[51] And it is often nice to be pampered, but when you look back at the most fun you have ever had, where were you? It is likely that you will remember days laughing with close friends, nights playing board games, a day at the beach, or that time you snuck into a party. Few of those scenarios were probably luxurious. Money opens up options and provides a safety net in case something goes wrong, but fun and excitement rarely have anything to do with money.

If you don't have much money, great—it doesn't matter. If you have a lot, wonderful—it doesn't make a big difference. The key as always is in following the EPIC model, because adventure is available to everyone.

---

51 Hilke Plassmann, John O'Doherty, Baba Shiv, and Antonio Rangel. "Marketing actions can modulate neural representations of experienced pleasantness." *Proceedings of the National Academy of Sciences of the USA,* vol. 105, no. 3, 1050–1054.

have ever been to this incredible eating establishment, you know we had a night of class and fine dining ahead. Dallas BBQ is the type of place where you can order a giant piña colada or a strawberry daiquiri with a double shot of Bacardi 151. Obviously this is where you want to take your most important clients or a date you want to impress.

Making our way past Greenwich Avenue, we saw an empty, bright orange, oversize Home Depot shopping cart. Scanning the area for the owner of the cart, we were clear it had been abandoned. So Roxie did the only logical thing: she jumped in and not so subtly hinted that we gentlemen would be pushing her around.

I loved her spontaneity and creative spirit. For my last birthday she and Zach told me they found the woman of my dreams, a tall blonde professional model they described as "the quiet type." Instead of bringing her to my birthday party, they gave me her lookbook. It was a collection of professionally photographed scenes involving a blonde blow-up doll. Needless to say I was in love, although it didn't really work out between us.

So we did as her royal coolness commanded. Roxie stood in the cart, arms out, as if she were a surfer riding atop her board. As a result of her stance, passing strangers began high-fiving this traveling anomaly. Meanwhile, JT and I took turns using every ounce of strength we had to prevent the cart from hitting people, parked cars, and oncoming traffic.

When we arrived at Dallas BBQ, we needed to park our ride. With no valet parking, only one option remained: buy a meter ticket for an hour, park the cart on the street, and get a window seat to make sure no one jacked our new ride.

The BBQ bartender, whom we had known since college, was standing outside and didn't even bat an eye at our entrance. You know you live a crazy life when your friends stop noticing your outlandish antics. After some ribs, mac and cheese, and a clogged artery or two, we needed a plan. Generally, I like to have a mission for the night, but I hadn't had the chance to plan anything, and that night we had the opportunity to try something new: we could roll around the city in our cart, impressing folks with our class and style.

Exiting this fine dining establishment, JT jumped in and we headed east. Our first stop was Continental, a dive on Third Avenue and St. Marks Place, to say hi to our friend Hitch, but it seemed that this new shopping

OBJECTS AND CATALYSTS

We have previously talked about how to dress and act to intrigue people, to draw them in and have them engage with you. Objects, pets, and exotic items can function in a similar way. What you carry with you or travel in is not only novel for you but works as a highly effective facilitator for conversation. Think about someone walking down the street with a beautiful dog. They probably don't have a dog because they want people to talk to them, but strangers are naturally drawn to and curious about things that stand out in a good way.

Before you leave home ask yourself: "Is there anything I can take with me that I am happy to carry and would add value to my adventure?" Watch out — the list can be endless, and you don't want to get stuck carrying things you don't want or need.

cart was so popular with strangers that we could barely get half a block without being stopped by people.

Making our way east on Eighth Street, we were spotted by a group of six girls dressed in matching fluorescent accessories and tiaras. They started screaming, "CART!" and ran at us with the intense excitement of children running to their presents on Christmas. JT was surrounded by these six screaming women grabbing at him as if he were a pop star being mauled by his fans. This cart was by far the stupidest and most effective catalyst for meeting people I have ever had. Somehow it had shattered the normal rules of behavior and social interaction. It had not only transported us around town but across social boundaries.

Realizing it was the bride-to-be's special night, Chris jumped out of the cart, and we helped her in and started pushing her around. "Stay here—

FEELING SPECIAL

There is a unique expression on people's faces when you have delighted them, when they feel like the center of attention and they neither expected it nor do they feel they deserve it. This wide-eyed look of joy is a gift. I would assert most people walk through life feeling ordinary, but if you can help someone feel special, it will be a memory they will cherish. I enjoy making people feel special, even strangers. I like the idea that I might not ever see that person again, but he or she will forever have a story of some guy who made his or her day or week through a random act of kindness. I encourage you to find a stranger and make him or her feel special. Who knows? You might be the highlight of that person's year.

we will be right back," I shouted to the group of women. Every person we passed cheered for her as she came by. She was a star, and it felt great to help her feel so special on the night of her bachelorette party.

When we returned to her friends, they adorned each of us with matching pink tiaras to say thank you. We graciously accepted. After all, we were already riding around in a bright orange shopping cart—how much more ridiculous could we look? It was time to move on. We had no interest in joining a bachelorette party. Over the years, I have taken over four of them, and I wasn't in the mood to babysit a group of strangers that night. We had a clear objective: continue exploring the city in the cart and make new friends.

Finally arriving at Continental, I was reminded what a dive this place was. It was so rundown you had to be careful where you stepped because it felt like the floor could give way at any moment. The nice thing about places like this is that they will let you get away with almost anything, which we proved when we slipped the bouncer $5 to bring the cart into the bar.

THE CELEB EXPERIENCE

You don't have to be famous to be treated like a celebrity; you just have to give people a reason to treat you special. If you walk into a bar dressed as a bride and groom, people will congratulate you, buy you drinks, and ask you questions. You're not famous, but you are being treated like a micro celeb.

Being a celebrity stems from social agreement. For whatever reason, society has deemed you worthy of attention. If you know how to draw that attention, hopefully for a positive reason, you can enjoy celebrity status.

There have been fun experiments in which ordinary people have hired fake paparazzi and cameramen to follow them around. As they did, strangers would walk up to them asking for photos and autographs and complimenting on their success. Some people would say what huge fans they were. This provides an incredible insight into the inner workings of fame. People will see you as famous if they have a reason to see you as famous. So if you want to be treated as a celebrity, just give people a reason to, regardless of whether it is real or not.

The bar was dimly lit and smelled of old beer. Doing our best to navigate the cart, we made our way to the back to surprise Hitch. When we found him, he jumped into the cart to hug JT. All the commotion caused the entire bar to look at us. JT, already a giant at 6-foot-4, stood in the cart towering over everyone and ordered a round. Even with the line at the bar two people deep, how could the bartender ignore him? The people standing at the bar cheered for JT, transforming him from patron to Lord of the Cart, a position worthy of applause and complimentary drinks.

With Hitch having to meet people elsewhere and the reek of old beer emanating from everything, it was time to move on and, more important, time for me to get a ride. Jumping into and standing in the cart, I could see the appeal. I stood two feet higher, my status elevated to Lord of the Cart, my minions doing my bidding and pushing me to my desired destination.

We thought we had found the epitome of social catalysts—a moving party of sorts capable of transporting a team of rabble-rousers—but as we crossed Second Avenue and Eighth Street, we realized we might have been outdone. Sitting on the street just off of the intersection was a dark green three-seater couch facing the passing traffic. Two men in their late thirties sat on it drinking beer they had bought at the bar behind them. Passersby would hop on the couch, chat with them, and then leave. They had taken transportation to a new level: instead of going from place to place to interact with interesting people, passing pedestrians would come to them, giving them new experiences and fun interactions. We knew we had to stay and hang out, so we parked our ride next to the couch, and while JT and Roxie introduced themselves, I went into the bar so we would have something we could toast these marvelous men with.

There we were: a ragtag group of adventurers, enjoying the most unlikely of situations. We sat for a moment in silence, enjoying the view of passing cars and shouts of recognition and approval from random strangers. It was a perfect moment in time, not for its beauty or even its camaraderie, but for its unlikeliness. When you venture forward and embrace adventurous opportunities, you can never predict exactly when you will have the pleasure enjoying these perfect moments.

It was approaching 2 AM, and no one wanted to do any more pushing. We decided it was time to park the cart again and relax somewhere a little quieter than a busy intersection. Roxie spotted a gorgeous Corvette parked on Eighth Street, and we figured that although our cart was worth a bit more, if it was safe enough for a Corvette, we could park our Home Depot shopping cart there.

Walking into the bar across the street, we experienced a sudden culture shock. Without the cart, we had been demoted from lords to peasants. No one even noticed us. We walked in expecting to be heralded for our outlandishness, but those few who saw us simply observed a girl and two slightly sweaty guys.

A BLANK SLATE

It is easy to forget that outside our element, outside the environment where people know us or about us, no one will necessarily care who we are. Of course, we are wonderful and people would love us if they only got to know us, but that is one of the gifts of and problems with exploration. The gift is that you can be anyone you want; the problem is that to everyone you are a blank slate, a nobody. People have to understand or be curious about who you are. It is the constant balance we have to find between relying on the past and creating the future. At times the familiar is fun and exciting; at others it is important to venture forward and create who you are.

Addicted to the attention and lifestyle the cart provided, we ran back to our ride, worried someone might have taken it. It was time to turn around and head back west. Once again, strangers shouted at us and ran up to us for rides. We were relieved that the magic had not been lost. In fact, the later it was in the night, the more people had drunk and the less inhibited they were to approach us. Our status had been restored. We had one last stunt to pull before we could go to bed. The only thing that could have made this night better would have been to have had Liam with us. Since he was staying in my apartment for a few weeks that summer, we thought we would bring the cart to him.

To pull this off, we would have to push the cart a mile west, get it into the subway, ride more than ten stops, bring it into my apartment, and somehow get it into his room without waking him. Riding inside the cart on the train was insanity. The constant jostling sent me from side to side, my head occasionally bouncing off of the poles riders hold on to. The looks and comments we got from strangers were priceless. When we finally made it home, Liam was nowhere to be found. So we did the only thing we could think of. We left the cart in his room with a note written in lipstick: "Should have been there . . . "

That evening, Roxie, JT and I went shopping for adventure. When Liam finally came back, we would deliver it, but that is a story best told in person. So if you ever meet me, make sure to ask.

It was an extraordinary night, and what made it so special was that we redefined our transportation as the activity. Rather than being a chore or necessity that we needed to deal with in order to have fun at the locations we wanted to go, we made it fun to go from place to place.

TAKEAWAYS:

☑ Transportation can be logistically complex. Mastery is achieved when you integrate the travel as an active part of the adventure.

☑ Unless you are heading to an event or a major destination, ten to fifteen minutes of travel time is the upper maximum between locations.

☑ There is no significant relationship between spending money and having fun. Living an adventurous life is attainable no matter how much money you have.

☑ Interesting objects can facilitate fun interactions with strangers. Carry something with you that helps you connect with others.

☑ If you want to be treated like a celebrity, you don't have to be famous; you just have to give people a reason to treat you like you are.

☑ Being unknown is both a gift and a source of discomfort. Even though the process of building trust can take time and effort, the freedom to recreate yourself is fun and exciting.

CHAPTER **16**

END WITH STYLE

YOU'RE OUT HAVING ONE OF THE most exciting first dates of your life. All you can think about is that you can't wait for the next time you get to see this person. Your night is coming to a close, and you are about to lean in for a kiss good-bye. Right before you do, your date says something so offensive that instantaneously all the magic is gone, and you never want to see that person again. In that moment, your night was ruined.

In reality, you had an incredible night except for a few seconds, but that's not how you will feel about it or remember it. It will exist as an awful memory that you avoid thinking about, but why? If we can have three hours of perfection and three seconds of misery at the end, why would we remember it as miserable?

It turns out that the likely way we process our enjoyment is based on a peak end rule. We don't process the duration of pleasure or pain; instead, we remember the peaks of an experience and how it ends. Furthermore, the way an experience ends is disproportionally valued.[52] This means that if you go out and have a mediocre night and end on an incredibly positive note, you will remember it much more fondly than if you have a great night that ends on a very bad note. Ending well is crutial to the positive memory of an event.

The implications of this knowledge to your enjoyment are significant. Most critically, it means that if you want to remember your experiences positively, make sure they have a few great moments and end with style. It is a careful trade-off: you may end an adventure prematurely rather than risk it deteriorating or ending on a sour note. Conversely, you may push further, believing you can create a night for the history books, but then fail. I have failed to end well more times than I can count. The number of pizza places I frequented at 4AM thinking it would be *awesome* is far more than I care to admit.

The next day I would wake up exhausted, annoyed at myself for staying out so late, remembering what would have otherwise been a great night as mediocre because I pushed to stay out long past the time I should have. As a result the next day was shot, spent in bed recuperating without having anything to show for it. After enough of these nights of wild adventures and unnoteworthy failures, the 2 AM principle finally kicked in. It always kept coming back to the fact that:

Nothing good happens after 2 AM, except for the most EPIC experiences of your life.

Unless you are wildly enjoying yourself or have a real reason to believe something exciting will happen later, when 2 AM hits, just go home. Odds are, the next day you won't be saying to yourself, "I wish I had been up at 5 AM last night," because almost nobody ever says that.

---

52 Daniel Kahneman, Barbara Fredrickson, Charles Schreiber, and Donald Redelmeier. "When More Pain is Preferred to Less: Adding a Better End." *Psychological Science*, November 1993, 401-405. pss.sagepub.com/content/4/6/401.abstract.

TAKE A LITTLE MORE PAIN. YOU WILL BE HAPPIER

Would you rather put your hand in uncomfortably cold water for a minute or a minute and a half? Which will you remember more or less fondly?

The legendary behavioral economist and psychologist Daniel Kahneman ran an experiment to see the effects of adding a better end to painful experiences. Imagine you participate in a study involving three activities[53]:

1. You put your hand in cold water—14°C (about 57°F) for sixty seconds, and as you do, you continually rate your discomfort.

2. You put your hand in the same 14°C water for ninety seconds, but during the last thirty seconds, the temperature is slowly increased to 15°C (59°F). Once again, you rate your discomfort throughout.

3. You have the choice of repeating either Activity 1 (sixty seconds) or Activity 2 (ninety seconds).

Which would you opt for, sixty seconds of discomfort or sixty seconds of the same discomfort plus thirty seconds of slightly less discomfort?

The overwhelming majority of people chose to repeat the longer option even though they experienced far more total discomfort. Fortunately for the participants, once they had made their selection of which activity to repeat, they were told they didn't have to repeat either.

---

53 Daniel Kahneman, et al. "When More Pain is Preferred to Less: Assing a Better End."

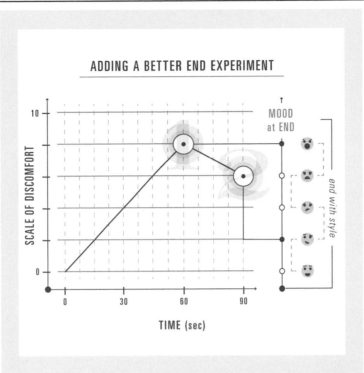

ADDING A BETTER END EXPERIMENT

The results suggest that the length of the experience plays a small part in the way it is remembered, but that the peak and the end heavily influence our memory.[54] Furthermore, it stands to reason that if you want to remember your experiences positively, focus on creating great peaks and ending very positively. A negative experience could be remembered less negatively, even positively, if you end well, and a positive experience can be remembered even more fondly by ending on a high note.

54 Ibid.

If you are going to keep going now, you know exactly what to do: follow the EPIC model.

THE EPIC MODEL OF ADVENTURE

STAGE 1	STAGE 2	STAGE 3	STAGE 4
ESTABLISH	PUSH BOUNDARIES	INCREASE	CONTINUE
Team Location Mission Constraints	Social Emotional Physical	Challenge Surprise Amuse Intrigue	Risk & Unpredictability Activity & Atmosphere Transportation End with Style

It will always be there to guide you every step of the way. You know now whom to take with you, where to go, how to push past your comfort zone, and how max out your enjoyment wherever you go. You even know where to go after and how to get there. If you do continue, make sure to go back to Stage II and repeat the cycle, until you end with style.

I have shared with you everything you need to know. You are now ready to live the adventurous life you deserve, and it is my turn to End With Style.

RIGHT HERE
RIGHT NOW

TODAY, THIS HOUR, RIGHT HERE, RIGHT NOW,
Earth or Near Orbit

Take a deep breath. Okay, now another. Seriously, I'll wait while you do.

We have been through a lot together since we started this journey. At the beginning, I promised that you would never see the world in the same way again and judging by everything we've covered, I'm sure we both agree.

I can't express how privileged I feel that you have trusted me with your attention for this long. In the next few minutes, it will be time for us to say good-bye—at least until we meet in person, and I wouldn't be surprised if we did. Don't worry: I'll be here any time you want to come back and relive how I embarrassed myself or convinced a stranger to do something insane, but now it is time for you to go out there and cause some trouble of your own. I know how uncomfortable that will be; in fact, I know how uncomfortable it is every day of my life.

I know I have probably never met you, but over the past few years as I knew this book was coming together, there were many times I was scared of a challenge or an idea I wanted to test, from talking to strangers and eating strange foods, to cliff diving and party crashing. I clearly recall occasions when friends would ask me if I wanted to do some outrageous stunt. After a brief pause I would say, "Absolutely not! Now let's go do it." During that pause I would remind myself that I can't expect you to push the limits of your comfort zone if I'm not willing to shatter mine. Frankly, most of the time I didn't want to do it, but that didn't stop me because you held me to a higher standard and I thank you for that. So before I go, I just want to tell you: You were fantastic. Absolutely fantastic. And you know what? Thanks to you, so was I.

Remember that the size of your life is proportional to how uncomfortable you are willing to be.

So I wish you a wonderfully uncomfortable life, and all the rewards that come with it.

Thank you for the honor and privilege. I raise my glass to you. I can't wait to hear about your adventures.

THE ADVENTURER'S ANTHEM

*(This is a reminder to all adventurers
of who we are and why we do what we do.)*

I have celebrated days when the sun never sets and nights where we fight dawn to our last breath. I know the exhaustion of sleeping on airport floors, bus seats, and park benches, and the fortune of beds fit for kings. I know the gift of a perfect night with a beautiful stranger and the fear of getting lost in a foreign land. I am friends with homeless prophets, the strangers at the next table over, the checkout person at duty-free, and even the koala in the Sydney Zoo. I have forgotten more outlandish experiences than most will have in a lifetime. I have flown more flights, ridden more miles, and sailed more seas in the pursuit of the absurd than any person before me. I know that it isn't the amount of time I live, but the number of memorable days I create; that my life is only as exciting as how uncomfortable I am willing to be; that I should never let a bull jump over me; and, most of all, that nothing good happens after 2 AM except for the most EPIC experiences of my life. I have had failures that would have crippled most, embarrassments that make me cringe, and injuries that I will never recover from, but through everything I laugh, knowing that the stories will live forever. After all, I am the greatest stranger you can't wait to meet, and when we cross paths, I will take you to places you never imagined and show you a world of opportunity in those you have been to a thousand times before. You'll challenge what is possible and discover the new person you can be. So if you want to live an exciting life, come and join me, but be prepared to grow, cause a show, and come out better than you know, because to live a life of wonder and adventure is a privilege, and we have to earn our right every day. So let's go.

TAKEAWAYS:

- ☑ Always end on a good note; it will define how you remember the experience.

- ☑ The EPIC model for adventure will always be there to guide you, so follow it.

- ☑ Nothing good happens after 2 AM, except for the most EPIC experiences of your life.

- ☑ If you ever forget who you are or why you put yourself through such craziness, remember the Adventurer Anthem.

SECRET ORIGINS

Those who know me know that I love heroes. Regardless of their source (mythology, comic books, movies, etc.), I find them inspiring. From the comic books I read growing up, it seemed that every hero's story begins with loss or tragedy. They are not born into success, but rather forged from experience. Each hero has a unique origin: Superman was sent to Earth from his dying planet to be a stranger in a new world; Batman was created when Bruce Wayne saw his parents killed in front of him; and Spiderman uses his powers for good after not stopping the criminal who went on to kill his uncle. Although I am no great hero, the science of adventure has its own secret origin, one that only a handful of people know. So here, for the first time, I share the full story.

40°48'16.8" N
73°44'7.2" W

SATURDAY, SPRING 1994, 8 PM GMT −5,

Somewhere on Long Island, New York, USA

I was thirteen years old, and much like many evenings in my childhood, my parents had dragged me to another adult party or social function. We entered a beautiful house somewhere on Long Island, and being the only teenager there, I sat alone on the side trying to entertain myself in an era before smart phones. If history had taught me anything I would be alone and bored the entire night, but in a moment of serendipity, my night took an unexpected turn.

You know those slow-motion moments in movies when the beautiful girl comes on-screen for the first time? Well it doesn't just happen in the movies. Her name was Natalie, and when she walked in, I was mesmerized. In the hours that we spoke that night, she charmed me.

At the end of the night, our families exchanged numbers and I was told to call. I was ecstatic.

Night after night, I sat in my room trying to build up the courage to call her, but I just couldn't. Months passed like this, until one night I managed to push my doubt and fear aside long enough to dial. The anticipation of hearing her voice was almost more than I could handle. In a moment I would be speaking to my dream girl. I held my breath, anticipating a ring, but instead, I heard a recorded message: "This number is no longer in service . . ."

My heart dropped. After battling all of the nervousness and insecurities and finally taking action, I had failed. My feelings had betrayed me, and now I had lost my chance. I sat there heartbroken, replaying all the internal conversations that had prevented me from acting sooner. In that moment, I made a decision: I would never let fear control me ever again. No matter how scared I was, I would have to take action. I would live a life beyond regrets.

As I grew up, I never forgot the promise I made to myself. I designed my life to be an adventure, in which fear became my driver to improve and grow. At times it led to great success and at others to embarrassing failures, but I never had to look back and wonder what if.

SPRING 1998
New York, New York, USA

40°44'08.3" N
74°00'24.1" W

I was seventeen years old and about to graduate high school. Soon I would be considered an adult, but what would that even mean? I didn't feel any different. Many of the adults I knew spent much of their time looking upset, anxious, or annoyed. Meanwhile, children engaged with the world in a very different way. They ran and played and got excited over *everything*! Unfortunately, somewhere along the line as we grow up, things go from wondrous to stressful. We trade a desire to explore for a desire to go back to bed. At some point, people trade a life of wonder and adventure for a life of mediocrity.

I wasn't interested in living life like that, so I figured that if I could embrace the way a child sees the world, with the same passion, I would lead a life I love.

I made a distinction between being childish and being immature. I believe that a person can be mature without letting go of their childlike wonder and adventurous spirit.

I found this philosophy embodied in the stories of "Peter Pan." So in honor of these great characters, I started a group called The Lost Boys, whose members dedicate themselves to living a life of childlike wonder and adventure. We became known for causing tomfoolery, shenanigans, and ballyhoo, but, above all else, honoring our word. As I shared the idea, the Lost Boys spread all over the world from the US to France, Australia, Israel, and beyond, and as it did, we changed the name to TLB so that anyone regardless of whether they were boys or girls could join.

But the story doesn't end there. You see, in the story of Peter Pan there is also a charming girl he met on one faithful night. Her name was Wendy Moira Angela Darling. As the story goes, no girl could hold Peter's eye quite like Wendy could.

When Peter and Wendy met for the first time, he had chased his shadow into her room. Wendy offered to sew his shadow back on him. As they sat there, Wendy was so charmed by Peter she asked if she could give him a kiss. Wendy leaned in to kiss him, Peter, being a naive boy, put his hands out expecting to be given something. Wendy, embarrassed by the situation, took the thimble from her pocket and put it in his hands. From then on, a thimble was known as a kiss.

In our TLB traditions, whenever there is someone who can hold our eye like no other, we give that person a token of our affection—a little silver thimble, a "kiss." One day, I hope to meet someone who can hold my eyes like no other, someone who deserves a "kiss." I'm sure she is out there.

Whenever I share the story, people always ask if I ever met Natalie again, and the answer is, "No, I never really tried." What resulted from meeting her was a wonderful experience that made me a better person. It was a story that ended with style and that is everything I could want. My hunch is I will bump into her one day, but I'm sure she would never remember the geeky boy she met at a party several decades before. Regardless, I owe her a debt of gratitude for changing her number; without that experience I would have had a very different life.

I end with a thank you to Natalie Hershlag:

From the boy who grew to become me, to the girl whom I met that night, I thank you for inspiring a life of adventure. For this I bestow upon you the highest gift and honor a Lost Boy can: You are now and forever a Wendy Lady, and as such there is a "kiss" that belongs to you as a token of appreciation. I can only hope that you grew up without ever growing old.

THE SCIENCE OF THE 2 AM PRINCIPLE

Although the EPIC model of adventure was informed by scientific research, it was built from the collection and examination of anecdotal data, and stories I came across or experienced. I want to clearly differentiate this from hard science or large-data science. When scientists run experiments, they attempt to control for every variable so that they can see if there is an actual relationship between things (e.g., does hunger affect test scores, does living in a city lead to more drug use, or is coffee healthy?). There are rigorous practices that we rely on to learn if there is a causation between these things.

When testing these ideas, scientists want to make sure that the conditions are the same every time the experiment is run. It would be difficult to discover the effect of hunger on test scores if a well-fed group took the test in a room where the temperature was 95 °F, and then a hungry group took the test in a room where it was 72 °F. Did the participants do better or worse because of the hunger or the temperature? To prevent problems like this from arising, researchers set standard conditions during their experiments so that they can arrive at empirical truths rather than collect useless and inaccurate data.

My process in developing the EPIC model of adventure was very different. Over the years people would talk to me about the most exciting experiences of their lives. When asked how their adventures happened, they typically attributed them to chance, believing they had been in the right place at the right time. I had a hard time believing that it was random chance when I noticed it was always the same friends that shared crazy stories, while other friends led wonderful but quiet lives.

If living an adventurous life was so consistent among certain people, I concluded that it must not be random. There had to be some qualities that these people embodied or traits they had, possibly ones they were unaware of, that led to a more adventurous life. I was convinced that if I could figure out what these were, I could discover a method to make our lives more exciting.

I began by collecting photos from my most remarkable nights out and looking for consistencies. Patterns became clear; stages emerged with specific characteristics in each, and from this a model was created, but I was still dealing with only my own experiences. I needed a larger data set, so I interviewed people and compared the model to their stories and tales of great adventures in literature. The insights I gained led me to simplify and reorganize my ideas.

Up until this point, my study was completely theoretical. If the EPIC model of adventure was going to be useful to anyone, it had to work when people were out socializing; it was time to have some fun, and fun was had. Over the course of more than two years, I went out and tested every stage and every characteristic, over and over again. My objective was not just to understand, but also to simplify. Antoine de Saint-Exupéry wrote in his book *Airman's Odyssey* that "perfection is achieved, not when there is nothing more to add, but when there is nothing left to take away." As a result, I was able to refine my theory down to the four-stage model that is the underlying premise for this book.

The EPIC model of adventure is not designed to encompass every possible scenario. Rather, it is meant to guide us through the complexities of living an adventurous life in a simple way that anyone can learn.

During these years of testing, I read research on human behavior and interviewed numerous scientists and specialists to understand what we know about the way we process excitement, emotion, memory, etc. These lessons are littered throughout the book, but instead of bogging you down with a lot of data, I have focused on including the selections that are the most applicable to your life and your adventures.

I have included this explanation to ensure that the EPIC model is not taken as hard science. It is not built on 100,000 carefully collected data points under laboratory conditions. Instead, it is based on my experiences and those of the people I spoke with in my research, and informed by countless stories and scientific research done by scientists far more brilliant than I.

The true test of a good model is if it works, and I can say, based on the countless days and nights that I have gone out and the hundreds of people I have come in contact with and taught this to, that you are in for a treat.

The EPIC Model of Adventure leads to an epic life!

ACKNOWLEDGMENTS

In Japanese, the word *yūgen* means "an awareness of the universe that triggers emotional responses too deep and powerful for words." I am disappointed that there is no similar word for gratitude. I can't express the enormity of the appreciation I have for the people who have supported me in going on these adventures and creating this book, and for those who have shaped me into the type of person who embraces such a full life. All I can do is describe the intense lump in my throat that prevents me from speaking, the welling up of tears in my eyes, which occasionally stream down and need to be wiped away, and a deep sense of being humbled and undeserving of so much love from so many. I will do my best to express my appreciation, but know that no words can sum up how I feel; it is "too deep and powerful for words."

MY FAMILY: If at the age of eight you had told this dyslexic, socially awkward child that he would write a book and create a life this good, I would have been convinced you were lying. But my parents Hanna and Benjamin; my siblings Ofer, Batsheva, and Amnon; and their spouses, Sharon and Shana, have always stood by me and supported me even when I didn't want it. When even learning to read one word was an overwhelming prospect and seeing a book brought on terror, you were by my side and we pushed through. I couldn't have asked for a better, more loving and supportive family. If I got to pick my family you would all be top of the list.

MY BEST FRIEND: Liam Alexander, I don't know why I deserve the friendship of such an extraordinary human being, I am just thankful that I can call you my best friend. You remind me every day what integrity is and what it is to live your values. Thank you for always saying "yes" and going along with my wild ideas and crazy adventures, and letting me participate in yours. You inspire me, and if I could pick my family, we would be related.

THE INSPIRER: *Hakshev* Zach Goelman! Not only did you have the first conversation with me that inspired this book, but you also showed me how to turn a miserable task, such as cleaning bathrooms, into a fun challenge. I am grateful for all you have taught me and for our years of friendship.

THE AGENT: Marc Gerald, thank you for seeing the potential in this scorpion-eating, cliff-jumping, bull-running troublemaker. Your experience and wisdom guided me through a process that scared and excited me more than you will ever know.

THE NAME: Kim Koba, thank you for giving my book such a cool name. It unified the ideas of the EPIC model and it created a phenomenal information gap. I have to say, you are very clever.

THE EDITORS: Lucas Wittmann, thank you for your continued support and feedback. From the moment we met I knew you were the editor I wanted for the project, and I couldn't be more proud of what we've created. Thank you for the phone calls at random hours while I was in cities I couldn't pronounce, trying to review stories with virtually no phone or Internet signal, and trying to get edits in before I would go off the grid to outlandish place's like Antarctica or the jungles of Panama. You were a gentleman and always supportive of my continued exploration, even when it made your work more difficult. Your team was wonderfully available. Max Anzilotti, your early feedback was clever and creative. Emily Greenwald, thank you for all your hours of edits and reviews over video Skype. I can't imagine it was easy considering the number of countries and time zones I called from. [Fun fact: the nice thing about Skype is that you don't necessarily have to be wearing pants, but you were wonderful enough to get dressed for the occasion; I, on the other hand, don't remember if I did.] Laura Hellman, you have read this book almost as many times as I have. Thank you for your obsessive grammatical nit-picking and dedication to the project. You went above and beyond anything I could have asked for and it was a treat to see you embodying the science and the principles socially. Gregory Henry, my publicist extradordinaire. Thank you for getting this book in front of the right people.

THE ESQs: Jesse Rosenblatt and Mike Gorenstein, not only are you two of my closest friends, you are fellow adventurers whose advice and legal support has kept me out of trouble so I could go cause some more.

THE FASHION ICON: Stacy London, to know you is to fall in love and to have a deep and profound respect and admiration for another human being. You embody the best our culture has to offer, making a topic that is intimidating accessible to everyone. You help us feel good about ourselves and you do it without a hint of anything but love. Thank you for your contributions and, more importantly, your friendship.

THE DESIGNERS: Paul Kepple and Max Vandenberg at Headcase Design. Thank you for the inspired design and the tireless effort to make this book the stunning product it is.

———————

THE PRODUCER: Daniel Laikind, I know of no one who puts as much thought into bringing extraordinary people together for fun times and interesting experiences as you do. Thank you for taking me on your travels and joining me on my adventures. From reviewing scientific research in the back of your car while on a US–Canada road trip to editing chapters in Buenos Aires after sneaking into a crypt, you have been a great friend and an exceptional troublemaker.

———————

THE PHOTOGRAPHER: Nick Onken, thank you for taking the time to photograph me. You are a great friend and an adored fellow adventurer. More importantly, you were able to make me look respectable, which is no small task. I tip my hat to you.

———————

THE SONG: When you spend months of your life traveling around the world typing stories while sitting in the beds of random Air BNBs, it helps to have a song to get you focused. I have lost count of how many times I have heard this one track on repeat while trying to stay in flow. Thank you, Helios for creating "Nothing It Can", and Spotify for your "Epic All-Nighter" playlist.

———————

THE BULL: Thank you for not killing me.

———————

THE DUTY-FREE CASHIER: Thank you for saying yes. My family and I adore you!

———————

THE LOST ADVENTURER: Victoria Nicodemus, as I wrote this book, you were taken from us in a tragic way. I have no words to express the deep loss your friends and loved ones feel. Your spirit lines the pages of these adventures and we will keep russelling up trouble in your honor!

———————

MY COMPANIONS: To all the people who befriended me, let me crash your parties, accepted my invitations, took me in when I had nowhere to go, stopped me from doing truly stupid things, and encouraged me to do even stupider things: You made the adventures worthwhile. Each and every one of you has a special place in my heart.

———————

MY FRIENDS: I have bounced around the idea of this book for so long, and so many of you have helped in ways that are immeasurable. I wish I could write full pages about how wonderful you are and how dear you are to me. Mary Pilon, Kelly Quann Bianucci, Chris Hazzard, Alec Colantonio-Ray, Seth Porges, Robbie Myers, Ariane Rockoff-Kirk, Jessica Banks, Jenna Ushkowitz, Kaj Larsen, Bill Phillips, Shane Snow, A.J. Jacobs, Tucker Max, Adam Vinokoor, Mike MacCombie, and Kirk Wagenbach. There are so many more of you I would like to thank. You know who you are. Some I can't say by name since you were part of my stories, some I can't say for many more fun reasons ;).

THE SCIENTISTS: Thank you to all who have dedicated yourselves to the endeavor of discovery and research. As every scientist builds on the work of the previous generation, there are more names to recognize than space to do so. I will keep it as concise as possible: Joseph LeDoux, James Fowler, Nicholas Christakis, Nico Bunzeck, Emrah Düzel, Edwin A. Locke, Barry Schwartz, Thomas Gilovich, Robert M. Yerkes, John D. Dodson, Matthew D. Lieberman, Jon Jecker, David Landy, Giles W. Story, Ivaylo Vlaev, Jonathan Oxford, Gregory S. Berns, Samuel M. McClure, George Loewenstein, Min Jeong Kang, Jesse J. Chandler, Emily Pronin, Marc G. Berman, John Jonides, Stephen Kaplan, Wilbert McKeachie, Thomas Goetz, Timothy D. Wilson, David Reinhard, Hilke Plassmann, John O'Doherty, Baba Shiv, Antonio Rangel, Daniel Kahneman, Barbara L. Fredrickson, A. Peter McGraw, Caleb Warren, Stephen Porges, Ueli Rutishauser, thank you all for your amazing work. Many of you were generous enough with your time to email with me and get on the phone to discuss your research and ensure your work was represented correctly in the pages of this book. I especially want to thank my close friends Moran Cerf, Janna Levin, Shep Doeleman, and my sister-in-law Sharon Levy for reviewing scientific papers and concepts with me. Your input was essential to my understanding of the material and ability to accurately express it.

THE UNSUNG HEROES:

There are many people who have had an unacknowledged impact on my life and this book, most of whom I have never had the privilege to meet. These people are deserving of far more than I can express, since they have had an impact on millions.

THE LEADER: As a child watching cartoons, one voice came through stronger than all the rest combined. It stood for all that was right and good in the universe. His name is Optimus Prime, leader of the Autobots from the Transformers TV shows and movies. He was voiced by the legendary Peter Cullen, and inspired a young boy to explore and wonder what secrets and possibilities the universe possessed. Peter, I know of no greater privilege I have had in my life than meeting you, and being inducted into the Autobots. You are everything a boy would want his hero to be. Thank you Tom DeSanto for making this dream come true and for bringing the *X-Men* and *Transformers* movies to life.

THE STORYTELLERS: Growing up on a healthy diet of cartoons and comic books, I was inspired daily by heroes who had a mission to protect those who could not protect themselves. They stood for doing what was right regardless of how difficult it was or what others would think. Thank you, Stan Lee for creating Marvel Comics, and Malcolm Wheeler-Nicholson for creating DC comics. As I adventure through life, I have not always been able to live up to these ideals, but they have given me a standard to strive for.

THE UNIFIER: In my childhood, being a geek meant being on the outskirts of society, but when Gareb Shamus created *Wizard*, the magazine that unified the comic-book industry and launched most of the events we know today as Comic Con, it gave us a sense of community and along with a few other major cultural events geeks were able to join the mainstream. We all owe y ou a debt of gratitude.

THE DOCTOR: I never felt truly connected to a hero until I discovered The Doctor. He travels through space and time, puts himself in incredibly uncomfortable situations, meets random strangers and takes them on epic adventures that change their lives for the better. That is all I ever wanted from life and, Russell T. Davies, you brought Dr. Who back to life for all of us to be inspired.

MOST IMPORTANTLY: Thank you to the force for being with me . . . always.

So far we met at least a doctor or two,
Named Matthew and Chris, and even named Who.
But one more than any I loved as a child.
He told stories so strange, so fun, and so wild.

He showed us what to do on a cold, cold wet day
When you sat there with Sally and just wanted to play.
He told us we can go any direction we choose,
for we have brains in our head and feet in our shoes.
So for Theodor Geisel who inspired my youth,
here's a story where you must discover the truth.

Now, let us begin at sixty below,
at a place that is cold and covered in snow.
It belongs to so many I can't even keep track,
like Agnes, Agatha, Jermaine, and Jack.
From the Brown point of this place for some time you will travel.
You will pass a cute dog that will make your stomach unravel.

North six o' five minutes and not any more,
at a speed that is equal to an average condor.
Here we will stop for a cocktail and food,
at what some would call "black pool" since it has a great mood.
We will have the house drink, and hear many tales,
from travelers who saw all the beautiful whales.

Next you head east and north quite a bit,
but who will we see? Are they known for their wit?
The ones that were fought for the island they claimed,
though some of them died and many were maimed.
Here we sit at five and enjoy the great high,
followed by fish that, as always, they fry.

continued . . .

The next day we cross that small pond to the west,
but bring all your money as you will want to invest.
This place is much smaller from whence you have come
with views of the mountains, a valley, and the sun.

Across a great ocean to the west is a place
where fat men do fight at a slow, graceful pace.
Once in this city a good friend of mine
dressed in a tutu and looked oh-so-fine.
Next to the south and east we will fly.
It will be many hours we spend in the sky.

Near the greatest canal man ever made,
you can use a Benjamin to buy and get paid.
It is 24 de Diciembre and for tomorrow's great day,
we travel to a land where many would pray.
It is the home of religions for so many people,
If you look at the capital you will see a church steeple,
and a dome, and a wall, and men dressed in black.
When we visit, militia will check your backpack.

There is only one place that is left in this tale.
If you paid attention I'm sure you won't fail.
Bring a costume with you to the last stop you make.
The water is warm and you'll enjoy a great steak.
Try as you mite the mar that they sell,
some think it heaven while I think it's hell.
You can sit and enjoy an opera so nice,
and a pale lager if that is your vice.

Now consider the travel that just did unfold,
did you keep track of all that was told?
If you have, then please answer the questions below,
but not with the public as they shouldn't know.
It would not be fair to ruin the surprise,
and remove any chance of them winning a prize.

So I present you now with the things that I need,
for you to be a winner when your answers I read:

*1. Assuming you travel like most readers can,
what day was it when this tale began?*

*2. If the laws of physics did not bend,
on what day would this story end?*

*3. What cities did you visit on this crazy trip,
and if I could have any, what would be my ship?*

*4. Most importantly tell me how adventurous you are.
This won't be easy as I set a high bar.*

*5. Tell me a story and entice me with it,
it better be honest I don't want your bull "spit."
If not a great tale, then inspire me now,
with the excitement you want, it need not be highbrow.*

So I await your great answers and I remind you once more,
keep this a secret, and you will enjoy what's in store.

About the Author

Jon Levy is a behavior scientist who studies influence and adventure. He specializes in applying the latest scientific research on human behavior, ranging from neuroscience and psychology to economics and biology, to transform the ways companies approach marketing, sales, influencers program development, consumer engagement, and product design. He is the founder of The Influencers, a private community comprised of over 800 thought leaders and tastemakers from across industries, ranging from Olympians, Nobel laureates, and members of royalty to celebrities, scientists, musicians and executives. To facilitate the development of the community, Jon created The Influencers Dinner, a private dinning experience where potential members congregate to cook dinner together and develop lifelong friendships.